ALANNA KNIGHT

Burke & Hare

the national archives

First published in 2007 by
The National Archives
Kew, Richmond
Surrey, TW9 4DU, UK

www.nationalarchives.gov.uk

The National Archives
brings together the Public Record Office,
Historical Manuscripts Commission,
Office of Public Sector Information
and Her Majesty's Stationery Office.

A catalogue card for this book is available from the British Library.

ISBN 978 1 905615 13 1

Cover illustration: portraits of (*left*) William Burke and (*right*) William Hare
(© 2004 Topham Picturepoint). Both practised deliberate murder
rather than stealing corpses from cemeteries (*centre*)
as ordinary 'bodysnatchers' did (Topfoto/HIP).
Jacket design by Goldust Design
Page design and typesetting by Ken Wilson | point 918
Picture research by Gwen Campbell
Printed in Germany by Bercker Graphischer Betreib GmbH & Co

Contents

—

Up the close and doon the stair
Ben the hoose wi' Burke and Hare,
Burke's the butcher, Hare's the thief
Knox the boy who buys the beef.

Children's song

———

Edinburgh's Dark Side

━━━

Edinburgh's history offers plenty of gory deaths. But, in the city's medieval Old Town in November 1827, the curtain was about to rise on a series of 16 murders so appalling that to this day they are equalled only by the multiple killings perpetrated in the early twenty-first century by Dr Harold Shipman. While late Georgian Edinburgh basked in its celebrated Age of Enlightenment, for the poor and destitute—the majority of its inhabitants—the city had its dark side, which was horrifically manifested in Burke and Hare's body trade.

It was a time of migration to the cities. In Scotland the construction of the Union Canal, linking the river Forth in Edinburgh with the Clyde in Glasgow, led to an enormous influx of workers. Among the thousands who crossed the sea from Ireland in 1818 were two unskilled labourers, William Burke and William Hare, to whom Edinburgh beckoned as a paradise after the poverty and desolation they had abandoned.

This city of tall houses and high-built narrow streets hosted a population explosion as the new flow of immigrants crowded into its heart. Accommodation was provided mainly by subdividing splendid old houses into one-roomed flats destined to be homes to whole families, and sleeping ten or twelve people. The inevitable overflow swallowed up the surrounding gardens of suburbs such as the Canongate and extended into the fields to the south side of Edinburgh, including Newington. The latter district was to become notorious as the location of No. 10 Surgeon's Square, the address to which Burke and Hare's corpses were delivered. And just a short distance away was the equally infamous 4 Newington Place, home of Dr Knox who bought the bodies for dissection.

Before the building of the New Town, English visitors to Edinburgh found the way that different social classes inhabited the same buildings remarkable. The typical residences were the tall tenements along the High Street, the Pleasance, Cowgate and West Bow and in the wynds and closes that led off them. Here social division was denoted not vertically but horizontally. The most respectable floors were generally the second and third, presumably because there one lived above the worst of the stench but only had a moderate number of steps to climb. In *Reekiana, or Minor Antiquities of Edinburgh,* R. Chambers describes one High Street tenement with a fishmonger's house on the ground floor accessible to customers, a respectable lodging house on the first and second, the rooms of the Dowager Countess of Balcarres on the third, a Mrs Buchan of Kelty on the fourth and above her 'the misses Elliott, milliners and mantua-makers'. Above them, the high garrets were occupied by 'a great variety of tailors and other tradesmen'.

The conditions in these Old Town human rabbit-warrens were an affront to the fastidious middle class, and the Edinburgh elite swiftly abandoned their homes in the tall 'lands' tenements when the New Town's Georgian streets and squares were built in 1767. This meant that by 1827 Edinburgh was in effect two separate towns. The Old Town sprawled along a spine of volcanic rock. Its High Street (the ruin of what remained of medieval Edinburgh and now known as the Royal Mile) has been compared to a gutted herring, with its head the Castle, its tail the Palace of Holyroodhouse and its bones the teeming closes and wynds. To the north across the Nor' Loch (now Waverley Railway Station, bordered by the Princes Street Gardens) lay the New Town, built to the classical design of James Craig. It was elegant and symmetrical, but offered what some thought a rather chilly splendour. Two masterpieces of engineering, the Mound and the North Bridge, connected the Old and New Towns.

Chambers went on to show how completely the building of the New Town served to redistribute the population according to class:

> The fine gentlemen who daily exhibit their foreign dresses and manners on Princes Street have no idea of a race of people who roost in the tall houses of the Lawnmarket and the West Bow and retain about them many of the primitive modes of life and

habits of thought that flourished among their grandfathers. Edinburgh is in fact two towns more ways than one. It contains an upper and an under town—the one a sort of thoroughfare for the children of business and fashion, the other a den of retreat for the poor, the diseased and the ignorant.

And it was to this 'under town' that Burke and Hare now belonged. In the wretched dwellings of rapidly formed ghettos, Irish labourers and other immigrants soon adopted the practice of taking in sub-tenants. In such overcrowded conditions, beds were an unnecessary refinement: tenants were not fussy about retiring each night in a whisky haze and sleeping on straw which had also been used by the livestock. It was also common practice for landlords who possessed a bed to take two lodgers to share it at a weekly rent.

By day washing hung out of tiny shuttered windows from which neighbours could shake hands (or fists) at each other across the narrow closes. Drains were unknown; by night those unfortunate enough to find themselves in these areas made their way through human and animal excrement as the cry of 'Gardy loo!' signalled the nightly emptying of chamber pots from the windows above. Robert Burns had his moment of cynicism when he named Edinburgh 'Auld Reekie' for its permanent pall of smoking chimneys. But the stink outside was nothing to that inside the narrow closes and wynds. Hygiene was a word not yet invented for the starving poor, and the stench would be unimaginable to our deodorized society.

The Irish brought with them the traditional 'wake', where a corpse awaiting burial was laid out for several days while money was collected to pay for the funeral. The family—often with eight or ten children—slept on dirty straw in the same room, amid the growing stench of putrefaction.

Despite these conditions, and the temptation presented to the starving poor by the combination of unlit streets and wealthy middle-class citizens, there was surprisingly little violent crime in Edinburgh before the advent of Burke and Hare. Until 1805, when the Edinburgh Police Act sent dedicated uniformed police to patrol the streets, law and order was the responsibility of a rather feeble town guard. It was ably assisted, however, by Edinburgh's 'caddies', who continued to exist alongside the new police: a brotherhood of unofficial guides who carried messages and letters, gave directions and recommended lodgings. These men were familiar with every address in town, and acted as a voluntary vigilante corps. On one occasion upon the council's instructions they caught and killed every dog in the city following an outbreak of rabies. Riots were another matter. The caddies were likely to be the first among the crowd if they thought popular justice was to be meted out. The composition of the mob varied according to its objectives, but it frequently included artisans and mechanics who were more middle than working class, and it was regarded by citizens as a means by which to rectify what they regarded as the grossest injustices. Dr Knox was to become just one of its victims.

GRAVE ROBBERS AND BODY SNATCHERS

In 1822 Edinburgh received a state visit from King George IV, stage-managed by the indefatigable Sir Walter Scott. As the decade wore on this state occasion was still a talking point over candlelit dining tables in the New Town. But by the late 1820s there was another topic on everyone's lips: grave robbers. At the time deaths were frequent even among the wealthy. Every wardrobe held black garments; there was always someone in mourning for a dear one, or for an infant born dead. And the grave was no longer a peaceful place: as darkness fell the grave robbers lurked, waiting for opportunities. Under the shadow of Arthur's Seat pinpoints of light over every kirkyard indicated the recently bereaved as they kept watch with lanterns. Rich and poor were united in this terrible nightly vigil. For the few who could afford it the 'mortsafe', a heavy iron grille which formed an impenetrable cage around the coffin, was available at the price of 1s per night. But the poor could resort only to a bottle of whisky or rum to keep out the cold and steady their nerves as they watched until dawn.

It is sad to be bereaved, but worse to have to guard over a loved one's grave. This was necessary night after night until the corpse could be assumed to have rotted beyond use on the dissecting table. And there was no one that the bereaved could trust, for the feared grave robbers were not only common criminals but often medical students, educated young gentlemen from well-off families, and therefore effectively endorsed by the establishment. They robbed graves not only for money, but to enable research that would ultimately benefit humankind.

Grave robbing was not a new phenomenon. The ancient Egyptians had their tombs robbed, as did the Romans, and in later centuries in Europe witches exhumed the corpses of children and executed criminals for their rituals. In Georgian Edinburgh it was a necessary evil rooted in the development of medicine as a modern science, a process promoted by the Napoleonic wars and the advance of industrialization. The tide of workers moving to take industrial employment in large cities caused a sharp increase in population, and the resulting overcrowding brought the spread of major diseases such as tuberculosis, typhus and smallpox. There were also industrial injuries caused by working with machinery—and industry depended on able bodied employees. So there was increased demand for doctors and surgeons, previously only consulted by the rich. For this demand to be met, the profession needed qualified teachers of anatomy.

Dr Robert Knox was one such. He began his career as Hospital Assistant to the Forces and attended the wounded on the battlefield at Waterloo. By 1827 he was the brilliant Surgeon Apothecary, Lecturer in Human and Comparative Anatomy at Edinburgh's Medical School. He was also a member of the Royal College of Surgeons of Edinburgh, with a lifetime appointment as Keeper and Conservator of its Museum.

Edinburgh's Medical School was part of its University and had been granted a charter to the Incorporation of Surgeons and Barbers in 1505. It was already famed as one of the finest training institutions in Europe and attracted many young men eager to become doctors, including Charles Darwin.

Certain anatomy teachers maintained that proper qualification as a surgeon required the dissection of at least three corpses. This was a tall order: the dearth of available bodies led to crowds of students scuffling around the dissecting table for a share of one corpse. As the gallows failed to supply enough criminals, the Medical School petitioned the town council for the right to dissect the bodies of suicides, foundlings who died in infancy and the unclaimed dead.

The Church was aghast at such a proposal. Christian Europe sanctioned only the dissection of the bodies of executed criminals, and in Calvinist Scotland pulpits thundered forth cries of outrage. Anatomists, they maintained, were depriving the poor of an afterlife. This was a time when the masses—rich and poor, sick and well—were sustained by a wholehearted and very literal belief in a Judgement Day.

The medical profession soon came up with a solution to its problem. Medical students in need of human material to further their research and complete their qualifications decided to find fresh subjects by 'fair means or foul'. And so 'resurrection men' —grave robbers or body snatchers—became an established aspect of everyday life in late Georgian Edinburgh.

It was a practice already long in operation in some parts of Europe, where there were no restrictions on the trade in bodies and doctors received the corpses of suicides and prostitutes as well as those of executed criminals. France on the other hand had never experienced any shortage of corpses, thanks to the efficiency of the guillotine, which for some time produced a daily and on occasion almost hourly delivery; its aristocracy sans heads supplemented unclaimed bodies drowned in the river Seine or found dead in the streets. Supply was so brisk that it exceeded demand and no more than five francs could be expected for a fresh corpse.

In Britain's major cities medical students were eager to seize upon this unique opportunity of importing corpses from France, and also from Ireland where no regulations existed. Cargos were landed in crates, their contents vaguely described as foodstuffs and marked 'urgent and perishable'. Unless the voyage was brief and distribution swift, the process of putrefaction led to gruesome discoveries of fast rotting corpses. In the absence of refrigeration, the corpse trade became a seasonal business. Winter corpses fetched a higher price than summer ones, because they could be kept longer without going off: the seasonal rate was £8 for summer and £10 for winter.

The domestic bodies trade presented its own challenges. It must be remembered that at the time burial clothes—gowns and petticoats for women and men's shirts and waistcoats— were not items to be worn once and then discarded. All clothes, and particularly shoes, were valuable commodities: even in rich families they were preserved and handed down. It was common practice even in the nineteenth century for a woman to put her wedding dress in a chest with strict instructions that she was to be buried in it. In the interests of speed and discretion, therefore, amateur body snatchers—primarily over-eager medical students—had to strip the body naked before removing it from the kirkyard, and often left behind piles of earth, broken coffin lids and shrouds to be discovered at daybreak. The alarm would then be raised, for although stealing a dead body which belonged to no one was a minor misdemeanour, the theft of shrouds or burial clothes from a coffin was a punishable crime.

In Edinburgh, resurrectionism became a profession of men who knew their business and were careful to leave a tidy churchyard, with soil and turf replaced and no evidence of open graves and broken coffins. This left them free to visit again. And the existence of this profession created an opportunity for villains like Burke and Hare. But, as Burke admitted at his trial, the pair were not grave robbers.

They were cold blooded killers.

CHAPTER ONE

Fresh Corpse for Sale

On the night of 29 November 1827, in a dire lodging house in Tanner's Close, two men huddled over the fire. Their solace against poverty and a bitter winter's night was drink. Whisky and rum could be obtained cheaply enough to guarantee a drunken stupor that would carry them through the dark hours until morning. Such a state would then be reinforced again as long as the money held out, so that in truth they were rarely completely sober even when awake.

William Hare—officially 'landlord', though the title is bizarre for the proprietor of such an establishment—lived there with his wife, Maggie Laird. William Burke and Helen McDougal (his wife only in Scottish law 'by habit and repute') had moved in earlier that month. The couples were of a similar age, and among the thousands of immigrant Irish navvies these two men who had never met in their native land were swiftly to become friends.

If this conjures up a picture of a convivial evening of couples sharing a laugh and a cheery drink, it could hardly be further from the truth. Drinking was an earnest business, essential for

survival and the temporary obliteration of despair, with work
regarded as a necessary evil to provide a daily supply of alcohol.

KILLERS IN THE MAKING

William Hare's early life in Ireland before he came to Scotland
is unknown. John Wilson, Professor of Moral Philosophy at
Edinburgh University, met the pair while they were in prison
and was shocked by Hare's sinister appearance. Writing under
the pen-name 'Christopher North' in *Blackwood's Magazine*,
he described Hare as 'illiterate and uncouth, a tall thin quarrel-
some, violent and amoral character with scars from old wounds
about his head and brow'. He continued:

> Hare was the most brutal man I have ever seen. His dull black-
> ish eyes, one rather higher than the other; his large thick or
> rather coarse lipped mouth; his high, broad cheekbones and
> sunken cheeks, each of which when he laughed—which he did
> often—collapsed into perpendicular hollows, shooting up
> ghastily [*sic*] from chin to cheekbone—all steeped in a sullen-
> ness and squalor not born of the jail but alive to the almost
> deformed face. The leering miscreant inspired not fear for the
> aspect was scarcely ferocious, but disgust and abhorrence, so
> utterly loathsome was the whole look of the reptile.

When his work on the Union Canal ended in 1822, Hare worked
as a labourer and met a man named Logue who ran a cheap

lodging house at the bottom of Tanner's Close, one of the squalid alleys in the West Port, near the local burial grounds. Its narrow, sunless passages lay between the walls of a dense conglomeration of slum tenements below the Castle mound, where the customary filth and dankness was aggravated by the stench of animal putrefaction from tanneries at the back of the 'lands' which gave the close its name. (Demolished in 1902, it was replaced by the present Argyll House.)

Logue's tenement had eight beds, and his charge of 3d a night did not limit him to taking lodgers eight at a time; more often than not, they slept three to a bed. Hare moved in, and took a fancy to Logue's common law wife, Margaret (Maggie) Laird. An Irish Catholic like himself, she had worked on the canal, digging in a navvy's jacket alongside the men. Described as 'a hard faced and debauched virago', she had a young child. No doubt Hare's friendship with her got him thrown out of the house, but in 1826 Logue died. Hare returned and installed himself at the Close, taking possession of house and widow.

By 1827, calling himself landlord and relieved of the need of employment, Hare occasionally worked as a labourer and, taking a step up the slums' social ladder, became a street vendor with a horse and cart from which he hawked fish and scrap about the Old Town. Most of his time, however, was spent drinking and fighting in public with Maggie, who was often intoxicated and seldom seen without a black eye.

Logue's Lodging, now Hare's, consisted of three rooms on

one floor of a stone-walled building with waste ground behind it. The eight beds were divided between the two larger rooms, and anyone passing by on Tanner's Close could see through the windows into both of these rooms. The third room was a smaller closet at the back with a window looking on to a wall and a shed or stall which appears to have served as a stable or pig sty (see plate 2).

This small room was to become the home of Hare's fellow killer. William Burke was born near Strabane in County Tyrone in 1792, the son of respectable Catholics; his father was a labourer. He had received a basic education, and in his youth served in the army and married Margaret Coleman—but he abandoned his wife and their two children to come to Scotland in 1818. During this period he met Helen or Nelly McDougal, a Scot from Redding near Falkirk. Described by North as 'an illiterate coarse woman' possibly earning a living as a prostitute among the canal navvies, Helen's surname was that of the man she was living with, by whom she had two children before abandoning them to follow Burke.

On the Canal's completion in 1822, Burke worked as an itinerant farm labourer and pedlar of old clothes around Peebles and Leith, where someone taught him cobbling skills. By 1827 he and Helen were in Edinburgh—where Burke's brother Constantine and family already lived—repairing old boots and shoes and hawking them among the city's poor. When they met Maggie Hare, who was an old acquaintance of Burke's, she mentioned Hare's spare room and suggested that Burke move in and carry out his cobbling trade. Burke eagerly seized this opportunity and the two men became friends, but there was no love lost between the two women: perhaps Helen was jealous of Maggie and Burke's prior acquaintance.

In the shambles of Hare's lodging house, Burke must have appeared a model occupant. This is suggested by Christopher North's description of his room:

> One of the neatest and snuggest little places I ever saw—walls
> well plastered and washed—a good wood floor—respectable
> fireplace—and light well-paned window. You reached the room
> by going along a comfortable and by no means dark passage
> about fifteen feet long—on each side of which was a room
> inhabited, the one by Mrs Law and the other by Mr & Mrs
> Connoway [who were to give evidence at Burke's trial].
> Another short passage, the only possible way of making it a
> room by itself and the character of the whole was that of com-
> fort and cheerfulness to a degree seldom seen in the dwellings
> of the poor. Burke's room therefore so far from being remote or
> solitary or adapted to murder was in the very heart of life, and
> no more like a den than any other room in Edinburgh.
>
> (See plate 6)

Given that this room was hidden from the outside, it was the most likely scene of the murders. Although criminal activities are usually associated with the hours of darkness, Hare's house at night would be crowded with lodgers sleeping two or three to a bed—so the murders must have been committed during the day when those same lodgers were absent, working or begging in the streets.

Burke was 37 at the time of the murders. This is Christopher North's description of him:

> A neat little man of about five feet five, well-proportioned, especially in his legs and thighs—round bodied but narrow chested —arms rather thin—small wrists, and a moderate sized hand, no mass of muscle anywhere about his limbs or frame, but vigorously necked, with hard forehead and cheek bones, a very active but not a powerful man, and intended by nature for a dancing master. Indeed he danced well, excelling in the Irish jig and when working about Peebles and Innerleithen he was very fond of that recreation. In that neighbourhood he was reckoned a good specimen of the Irish character—not quarrelsome, expert with the spade and a pleasant enough companion over a jug of toddy. Nothing repulsive about him, to ordinary observers at least, and certainly not deficient in intelligence.

On first acquaintance Burke would also have found favour with Sir Walter Scott, who said in his *Journals*:

> Our canals, our railroads, our various public works are all wrought by Irish. I have often employed them myself, for burning clay and similar operations and have found these labourers quiet and tractable, light spirited too, and happy to a degree beyond belief, and in no degree quarrelsome, keep whisky from them and them from whisky.

However, he went on to warn that:

most unhappily for all parties they work for far too low a rate—
—a rate in short which can but just procure sale and potatoes;
they become reckless of course, of all the comforts and decen-
cies of life, which they have no means of procuring. Extreme
poverty brings ignorance and vice and these are theatres of
crime.

To all outward appearances, including sketches made of him in
prison, Burke appears a more agreeable and sociable character
than his friend Hare, whose sinister appearance and violent
character would not have fitted so neatly with Sir Walter's
favourable opinion of the Irish.

There is little recorded of credit to Mrs Burke and Mrs
Hare. According to North they were 'Poor, miserable, bony,
skinny, scranky, wizened jades both, without the most distant
approach to goodlookingness. Peevish, sulky, savage and cruel
and evidently familiar from earliest life with all the woe and
wretchedness of guilt and pollution.' Mrs Hare 'had most of the
she-devil' and was a cleverer woman than Mrs Burke, who was
'of a dour and sullen disposition, morosely jealous and gloomily
wicked'.

Further to their detriment, it is almost impossible to believe
that these two women were ignorant of what was taking place
in their homes. Perhaps they not only helped to procure 'subjects' but stood by while their men murdered 16 innocent victims, including a young boy and a beautiful girl.

AN OLD MAN DIES...

Burke and Helen had scarcely settled into Tanner's Close in 1827 when Hare discovered that another lodger, an old man named Donald, had just died of dropsy. For Hare this was a disaster: the old man owed him £4 in rent and his quarterly army pension, due shortly, would have covered the debt.

It was impossible to be part of the Edinburgh underworld at that time and not know that there was a lucrative trade in selling corpses as anatomical subjects. In the slums adjacent to the High Street and Canongate, four professional resurrection men were well known to the locals and to the medical students at Surgeon's Square. The most infamous was Andrew Merrilees, 'Merry Andrew', whose nickname was belied by his death's head appearance. According to Andrew Leighton's description in *The Court of Casus*:

> He was of gigantic height, thin and gaunt, with a long pale face, and the jaws of an ogre. His shabby clothes, no doubt made for some tall person of proportionate girth, hung upon his sharp joints more as if they had been placed there to dry than to clothe and keep him warm. No less grotesque were the motions and gestures of this strange being. It seemed as if he went upon springs, and even the muscles of his face, as they passed from the grin of idiot pleasure to the scowl of anger, seemed to obey a similar power.

His associates were called Spune, Stupe and Moudiewarp (Scots for Mole), their names based on their facility in their trade. They were occasionally joined by a lugubrious mock minister known as Praying Howard; he specialized in pauper funerals, at which he marked down bodies for future use.

At the merest whisper of the deathbed of a friendless vagrant, this grisly quartet would hasten forth, hoping that the unfortunate's dying words would reveal information enabling them to reappear disguised as relatives. If this was successful, Merry Andrew would deliver a eulogy on the deceased's virtues and return with a coffin and cart to remove the body to the family burial place. Once the corpse was safely on board, it was swiftly removed from the coffin, stripped of its shroud and delivered to No. 10 Surgeon's Square.

It occurred—probably to the crafty Hare—that he and Burke could benefit from this trade. Donald had no friends or relations, so here was an unclaimed fresh corpse ready for sale which could fetch up to £10. Think of the drink they could buy, and clothes for their women. Hare promised Burke a share of the proceeds for his assistance, and if Burke—a pious man even on the scaffold—ever knew a moment's doubt, he was soon persuaded by greed.

Hare moved fast. Preparations were made for the old man's burial by the parish and the body was placed in a coffin ready for the hired mourners known in Scotland as 'saulies'. Then Hare forced open the coffin, and the two men lifted out the corpse, hid it in a bed and filled the coffin with tanner's bark from the yard at the back. Its lid having been firmly refixed, the coffin was taken from the house and with brief solemnity interred in a pauper's grave in the kirkyard of St Cuthbert's a quarter of a mile away.

Relieved that all had gone smoothly so far, the two men then walked the half mile from Tanner's Close to the Old College on the South Bridge. Meeting a young man they presumed to be a student, they asked to be directed to Dr (later Professor) Monro's rooms.

How did they know who to ask for? The leaders of late Georgian society in Edinburgh were the professional classes: the lawyers and doctors. Graduates of the Medical School had immense prestige, due in no small measure to the professional dynasty of Monros, three generations of whom held the Chair of Anatomy from 1720 to 1846. Alexander Monro the third was already a legend in his own lifetime. Everyone had heard of him, even Edinburgh's underworld, and perhaps a whisper among the resurrectionists overheard by Burke or Hare had suggested Monro as a buyer of Donald's corpse.

Neither Hare nor Burke were particularly articulate at explaining their mission to the student at Dr Monro's door. When at last he prised out of them the delicate nature of their errand, the student, who was a pupil of a rival anatomist, advised them to try Dr Robert Knox's establishment at No. 10 Surgeon's Square, a short walk away.

Surgeon's Square was an imposing building which housed

the Medical School's lecturers' rooms. It was situated near the old Infirmary, which had a small and convenient burial place for unclaimed patients. By day it was noisy and bustling, with six lecturers in anatomy demonstrating to crowded classes of students. When night fell upon the empty classrooms with their eerily shrouded dissecting tables, the silence was broken only by the stealthy tread of individuals whose business it was to provide fresh human material for the next day.

Having at last found the rooms, Burke and Hare were met by three young men—William Fergusson, Alexander Miller and Thomas Wharton Jones. The visitors were apparently new to the corpse trade and unknown at Surgeon's Square, but at last, after some shuffling and mumbling, it emerged that they had a dead body for sale. Burke and Hare learned with surprise and gratification that such commodities could fetch as much as £10, and promised to return with their 'package'. They were not asked whose body it was nor how they had obtained it.

Gleefully returning to Tanner's Close, they stuffed Donald's corpse into a sack and, impatiently waiting until Edinburgh slept, returned to Surgeon's Square that night. They were greeted by the same three students, who happened to be on the night duty rota, and told to bring the body upstairs to the lecture room. There it was laid on the dissecting table, still dressed in its burial shirt.

Burke and Hare were sternly told to remove the shirt at once and take it away. This they did, to the watching students' evident relief; as Dr Knox's assistants, used to receiving corpses from body snatchers, they would have been well versed in the law concerning clothes and other property. Dead bodies were always sold naked; Georgian criminals were very particular about this.

ENTER DR KNOX

By chance, as Burke and Hare were removing the dead man's shirt, Dr Knox entered the room. Looking at the naked corpse, he suggested a payment of £7 10s. This being readily agreed by Burke and Hare, the doctor told Jones to settle with them. Hare took £4 5s and gave Burke £3 5s, and they were shown off the premises; one of the students said they would be glad to see them again with another body.

The great Dr Knox then returned to his comfortable home at 4 Newington Place, a short distance away, unaware that the scene he had left at Surgeon's Square had decided his fate. If Burke and Hare had not by chance been directed to his establishment, the odium which fell upon him would have attached to his rival, Dr Monro.

John Robert Knox was born in 1793 into farming stock, and was keen to claim kinship with John Knox the Reformer. He grew up to be known in Scottish parlance as 'a lad of pairts', a brilliant scholar from a humble background. After obtaining his degree in anatomy and surgery, he went to London to finish his education as a pupil of John Abernethy at St Bartholomew's Hospital, and from 1815 served in the Napoleonic Wars as Hospital Assistant to the Forces.

With a soldierly bearing, powerful shoulders and long arms, he must have relished the plumed hat and long sword worn by the army surgeons. He was always something of a dandy, as described by his biographer and former pupil Henry Lonsdale in *A Sketch of the Life and Writings of Robert Knox the Anatomist*: 'With spotless linen, frill and lace, and jewellery redolent of a duchess's boudoir, standing in a classroom amid osseous forms, cadavers and decaying moralities, he was a sight to behold and one assuredly never to be forgotten.' This spectacular appearance did not extend to his face. Smallpox in childhood had coarsened his skin and features, and his eye had atrophied, leaving only the socket. His students nicknamed him 'Old Cyclops'. But fate had compensated with a melodious voice and great personal charm. His talks enthralled audiences and women found him attractive.

Knox returned to resume his life as an Edinburgh doctor, settling first with his family in Nicholson Square and when married moving to Newington Place. Little is known about that marriage, although it seemed happy enough: nobody ever met Mrs Knox or knew her name. The hints are that Knox had married beneath him; if his wife was, for example, a domestic servant, then he perhaps did her a kindness by protecting her from class conscious Edinburgh society.

Dr Moores Ball in *The Sack'em Up Men* described Knox as:

> A great strong outstanding and a brilliant character, the most
> eloquent, the most versatile and the most thorough teacher of
> anatomy that Scotland, a country which long has been noted for
> the excellence of its anatomical instruction ever has produced:
> Robert Knox—he who was designated as *Knox, primus et
> incomparabilis* had his life wrecked, ruined and embittered for
> the fortuitous circumstances which caused the murderers
> Burke and Hare to cross his path.

But Knox knew the score. The corpse trade was a black one, but
it existed and was there for him to make use of. He did not hesitate: as a successful man who never begrudged money spent to
further his art, Knox decided to outbid his rivals. In a single
year, he was reputed to have spent over £700 to ensure that his
dissecting rooms were never bare. On one occasion, Lonsdale
states, Knox 'actually paid 25 guineas rather than see his class
disappointed'—a vast sum, and more than double the usual
price. Knox was in touch with the resurrectionists in Dublin and
London, and was widely known as a reliable employer who paid
cash on delivery. Once he made a boast, which with hindsight
might have been better left unsaid, that he could 'always com-
mand subjects'. Knox meant simply that he was prepared to
pay the maximum price to ensure supply, but this statement
was seized upon by his enemies to mean that he had the West
Port villains in his pay.

When the resurrectionists made their deliveries, Dr Knox was usually prudently absent, and he was rarely at Surgeon's Square after hours. His three senior student assistants worked a rota system with a porter, David Paterson, who was on duty all night. Paterson, who tried to push himself into the limelight at Burke's trial by claiming to be 'Keeper of the Museum' of the Royal College of Surgeons, had only recently entered Knox's service. As a porter earning a wage of 7s a week he was not above trying to do a dishonest deal with the resurrectionists or body snatchers. His duties were daily cleaning of the rooms, keeping the door, running errands and receiving 'packages'. He took down the names of the men who brought them—rarely their real names—and the date the corpses were received. He claimed to have had orders from the doctor 'not to interfere at all with these men' (*Echoes of Surgeon's Square*, 1829).

Much has been made of this statement, and it was seized upon as proof of Knox's complicity in the Burke and Hare murders—whereas it could be accepted as a quite necessary precaution. If too much curiosity had been shown in the resurrectionists' affairs, they might have taken their trade elsewhere.

Once the 'package' was inside the house, the three students noted its age, sex and general applicability to the requirements of the class. If suitable, the corpse was accepted and the seasonal payment made. The body was then consigned to a cold damp cellar, and the next day placed on the dissecting table in readiness for Dr Knox's demonstration.

In this matter Knox was simply following the accepted procedures of the time. These channels for the supply of subjects were employed by every surgeon in Great Britain. Knox put the most responsible students in charge of his room: Fergusson, who became Sir William Fergusson, Sergeant-Surgeon to the Queen and President of the Royal College of Surgeons of England; Jones, later Professor Thomas Wharton Jones of University College, London; and Alexander Miller, who was to become an eminent surgeon.

When Burke and Hare returned to Tanner's Close that night, they were no doubt jubilant. What an opportunity! And so it all began: they had taken the first steps on a destructive journey. Winter lay ahead, but with the passing days the money they had received for that dead lodger began to haunt them. Such easy money… Why not keep their ears and eyes open for news of the dying, and move in quickly before the professional body snatchers? Their own lodgers were another potential source, particularly the elderly, sick and ailing. Why not help them out and at the same time help themselves?

As the winter days passed, Burke and Hare had a long wait for another opportunity, but in February 1828 they got lucky again. Another lodger at Tanner's Close died—this time with their assistance.

CHAPTER TWO

Serial Killers at Large

What was going on in the minds of Burke and Hare during the three months between the sale of their first and second corpses? Did they brood on that £7 10s they had received for Donald's corpse until it became an obsession? Perhaps—especially when there was no money for drink—they considered joining the ranks of the professional body snatchers. If so, doubtless they soon rejected that idea: neither was addicted to hard work or fancied the risky business of robbing graves, and security measures in Edinburgh's burial grounds had been tightened. Body snatchers not only faced the exhausting business of digging in graveyards guarded by mortsafes, watch houses and booby-traps while being shot at by the guardians of the bereaved; sometimes they had to bribe undertakers and watchmen. And Burke and Hare, having no transport, would have had to carry bodies from remote churchyards.

Hare kept a sharp eye on his lodgers for signs of sickness that might prove fatal. At last one named Joseph, a miller before his retirement, fell ill with a fever. The precise nature of his condition was unknown; when he became delirious, Hare's first concern was that he might scare off the other lodgers. Cholera and typhus were endemic, a constant terror, and spread very rapidly in Edinburgh's slums. Joseph's fever would empty those other beds that guaranteed a minimum income of 2s a day. However, a quick calculation told Burke and Hare that this was a miserable income compared with the riches to be earned by selling a body.

They watched Joseph intently. Burke remarked in one of his confessions that Joseph had been known to be previously well off and well connected. If he was reduced to lodging with Hare, it suggested that he had fallen on hard times, and had no close ties. His condition was doubtless a subject of constant speculation before Burke and Hare eventually reached the decision that if he was going to die anyway, why not relieve the poor fellow of his earthly sufferings?

They decided to be generous with the whisky supply, which in Joseph's feeble condition soon rendered him unconscious. He was in no state to fight against the pillow thrust over his face by one while the other lay across his body to prevent him struggling and making a noise. Soon it was over, and after dark the two killers carried Joseph's body to Surgeon's Square, where they were once again met by Dr Knox's three students and asked to lay out the corpse. This time, remembering the rules, they had behaved like professionals and stripped the old man naked.

After the students had taken a quick look, Burke and Hare were paid the winter rate and no questions asked. Again they could hardly believe their good fortune in discovering such a gold mine. It was so easy: a steady supply of corpses guaranteed an unending supply of drinks, and all for saving some old fellow from the misery of a prolonged deathbed.

As for considering the enormity of having taken a life, Burke was probably intelligent enough to tell his conscience that they were benefiting medical science. He was to say in his prison confession that he had not 'the smallest suspicion of any other person in this, or any other country, except Hare and himself, being concerned in killing persons and offering their bodies for dissection and that he never knew or heard of such a thing having been done before'.

The fact remains that they had got away with murder. Heartened by success, they lost no time in finding their next victim. An English street vendor who sold matches or tinder on the Edinburgh streets was seeking a few nights' cheap lodging. Perhaps he was already ill, for almost immediately upon his arrival at Hare's establishment he went down with jaundice. Again, Hare regarded this as a threat to his lodgers and again he and Burke could not resist the temptation to kill. They did not hesitate. Out came the whisky bottle and down came the smothering pillow. Soon they were collecting another £10 from Surgeon's Square.

However, given their lifestyle, this ill-gotten money soon disappeared. Burke and Hare were presented with a problem. They had been lucky to have two lodgers in poor health who were probably going to die anyway, but they could hardly expect this state of affairs to continue. Lodgers wouldn't keep falling ill; even if they did, in the better weather they might recover.

The success of the pair's previous efforts must have made them feel infallible. Their money obsession was now like a drug habit and they were prepared to go to any lengths to feed it. They took their first great risk.

This time their victim was an old woman, Abigail Simpson, whose former employer allowed her a weekly pension of 1s 6d and a can of dripping. To collect it she regularly walked into Edinburgh from Gilmerton, a few miles to the south, and to supplement this pathetically meagre income she sold salt and kaolin (or pipe clay, popular among servants for whitening doorsteps) while she was in the city.

On 11 February, according to Burke's confessions, he spotted her hawking her wares in the street. Inviting her to Tanner's Close, he got her so drunk that she was unable to return home to Gilmerton or anywhere else. She told Hare she had a daughter, to which Hare responded that as he was a single man he would marry her and take care of them both. Next morning, hardly surprisingly, she felt ill and was very sick, but was persuaded to take 'the hair of the dog'. Hare came in and looked down at her lying insensible on her back in bed, dressed in 'a drab mantle, a white-grounded cotton shawl and small blue spots on it'—an item produced as evidence at the trial. Here was a 'shot' (body snatchers' slang for a corpse). They should smother her and sell her body to the anatomists.

This method of dealing with their victims by first drinking heavily with them, reducing them to unconsciousness, was to become Burke and Hare's regular preparation for murder. It had the advantage of giving the two killers courage they might have lacked if sober. The picture it conjures up is appalling. Even though drunk, the victims must have been aware that they were being murdered, and must have struggled, but in the knowledge that they were incapable of fighting for their lives against such a pair.

Burke and Hare went to work on Abigail Simpson immediately. Burke lay across her while Hare clapped his hands over her mouth and nose to keep her from making a noise. Soon it was all over. Abigail was dead, her life snuffed out for a few pence and a can of dripping. She was undressed and her body put in a tea chest. As it was still daylight, Burke and Hare walked to Surgeon's Square to inform Dr Knox's assistants that they had another subject. Mr Miller agreed to send a porter to meet them that evening at a spot below the Castle Rock. Burke and Hare took the chest there as promised, and accompanied the porter who carried it to Surgeon's Square. The corpse was cold and stiff when Dr Knox came in to inspect it; he approved of it being so fresh, Burke was to say later, but did not ask any questions. They were paid £10.

Doubtless Dr Knox and his assistants were eager to purchase corpses, and used to accepting them, but three fresh subjects from the same two men in as many weeks begs the question why they did not ask about the source of the bodies, or confide any suspicions to one another. Perhaps their dedication to medical science blinded them to other issues. All we have to rely on are the statements of Burke and Hare, which differ even regarding the sequence in which the murders were committed. According to Burke's confession, after the death of Donald they did not try anything like it again for three months. He also claimed that he and Hare 'often said to one another that no person could find them out, no one being present at the murders but themselves two; and that they might be as well hanged for a sheep as a lamb'.

Two old lodgers, beggars or derelicts, might well have gone unnoticed, but Abigail's disappearance would surely have been remarked upon, at the very least by the daughter she had boasted about. In her case Burke and Hare had seemingly been too eager for financial gain to consider the possibility that there might be anxious relatives. Emboldened by their success—the money and encouragement from Knox's assistants—they wanted more bodies to sell, and when March came and went without any 'shots', desperation led them to take a massive risk on their next victim.

THE FATE OF MARY PATERSON

On Wednesday 12 April, Burke was drinking rum and bitters in William Swanston's grog shop in the Canongate when two prostitutes came in. Janet Brown and Mary Paterson, also known as Mitchell, were both in their late teens and were well known on the city streets. Mary in particular was a strikingly good-looking girl, though that day she had curling papers in her hair; orphaned in childhood, she had turned to prostitution to survive. That morning both girls had emerged from the Canongate watch house where they had been detained by the police for some disturbance of the peace. On their release they had first visited Mrs Lawrie, their former landlady in Leith Street, the notorious red light area of Edinburgh, although they were now lodging with Mrs Burnett or Worthington in the same street. Doubtless both women were brothel keepers and the girls were seeking advice and new customers.

Burke knew the girls and their reputation, and his genial greeting was followed by three gills of rum and bitters furnished at his expense. Listening sympathetically to their tale of woe about the local police, he invited them to breakfast at his lodgings nearby. Mary, bolder and more impulsive than her companion, was easily persuaded, but her friend Janet was less eager. However, she was won over by Mary's urging and flattery and extravagant promises from Burke, including the lure of a pension with which he could keep her handsomely for life.

All three left the gin shop with two bottles of whisky, but instead of walking the girls to Tanner's Close, Burke led them to his brother Constantine's home in nearby Gibb's Close, informing them that he was at present lodging there. Already forming a fiendish plan for the pair, Burke was taking care to avoid Mary or Janet being seen in his company.

Constantine's house, accessed via a dark passage and a narrow staircase, turned out to be a depressing single room. The bed, hung with tattered curtains, was at that moment occupied by Constantine and his wife Elizabeth, a truckle bed alongside doubtless for their sons. Anxious to conceal his relationship with the couple, Burke played the part of lodger, indignant at their laziness and neglect. Elizabeth got up, kindled the fire and in due course provided a good Scots breakfast for the unexpected visitors. They washed down eggs, bread and smoked haddock with tea and the all-important whisky.

By the time Constantine left for work, the two bottles were almost empty and Mary was in a drunken slumber over the breakfast table. Regarding her with satisfaction as almost certain prey, Burke turned his attentions to Janet who, to his consternation, was less affected by the whisky and still wide awake. Burke persuaded her to go out with him for a breath of air, escorting her to a nearby tavern where he plied her with pies and porter before taking her back to Gibb's Close.

As they sat down at the table to consume the remains of the whisky, the bed curtains flew open to reveal the angry features of Burke's wife. She had called while Burke was absent to find the young and attractive Mary Paterson drunk and fast asleep. Elizabeth had told her that her husband had gone out with another girl. During the altercation that followed, Helen tried in vain to stir the sleeping Mary, then turned her attentions to Janet. She was restrained from violence only by Burke's inter-vention, while Janet apologized in the background that she had not known Burke was married. A brawl ensued, in the course of which Burke threw a glass at Helen, cutting her forehead. He then pushed her out of the room and locked the door behind her.

Left alone with Janet, Burke found that lust had taken tem-porary ascendancy over his desire to murder, but she refused to be coaxed into bed by his Irish charm and insisted on leaving immediately—with good reason, as Helen was furiously ham-mering on the other side of the door. A disappointed Burke escorted her past the screaming virago at the stairhead, urging her to return later. She promised to do so, but deciding that she had had a narrow escape from Mrs Burke, hurried back to Mrs Lawrie's house in Leith Street.

Elizabeth Burke meanwhile had gone in search of Hare. When the two returned along with Mrs Hare, the three wives were told to wait outside the room. Locking the door on them, Burke and Hare got down to business. They laid the uncon-scious Mary on the bed, where they had no trouble in smother-ing her in the usual way, putting an end to her short life. Burke went at once to Surgeon's Square to arrange another delivery.

While he was gone, Janet Brown turned up again, still in a whisky haze, with Mrs Lawrie's servant girl and strict instructions that she was to collect Mary and return immediately. Her reappearance sent Helen, now assisted by Maggie Hare, into a wild fury. This time Hare intervened, telling Janet that Burke had gone for a walk with Mary and would be back shortly. He asked her to send the servant home so they could have a drink together.

One shudders to think how close Janet Brown was to death during those few minutes, drinking whisky with the genial Hare and the three scowling women while her friend Mary lay murdered a few feet away—and with Burke due back any moment to pack up the corpse for Dr Knox. It is impossible to believe that the three women, Maggie Hare, Helen Burke and Elizabeth Burke, were ignorant of what lay hidden by the bed curtains, or to imagine that they were not accomplices in the plot to abduct and murder Janet.

While all this was going on, Mrs Lawrie sent the servant back for Janet, who left, little guessing that she had been marked down as the next corpse for sale, and then returned, as she had promised Hare. This time she was met by Elizabeth Burke who sent her away, saying that Burke and Mary had not returned. Janet left again—and never in the short history of Burke and Hare's victims had there been such a narrow escape.

Inside the house Burke and Hare had stuffed Mary's corpse into a tea chest. Burke was not keen to leave it there until dark, for Constantine to find when he came home from work, so reluctantly they carried the box straight to Surgeon's Square. It must have been a less than happy journey: at the High School Yards they were greeted by schoolboys who followed them, pointing and chanting 'They're carrying a corpse!'

Burke and Hare were admitted to Dr Knox's rooms by Mr Fergusson and another lad. However this time they were in trouble, because the lad seemed to recognize Mary's body. He and Fergusson asked where it had come from, and Burke explained that he had bought it from an old woman at the back of the Canongate who said the girl had killed herself with drink.

Dr Knox's doorkeeper David Paterson (no relation to Mary) arrived to find Miller talking to Burke and Hare with a female subject on the floor. He heard Fergusson say that he was acquainted with the deceased. Paterson handed over £8 for the body and the students asked Burke and Hare to cut off the girl's hair, which still had her curling papers in it. One handed Burke a pair of scissors; she was warm when he used them.

Later, when Burke came on another errand, Paterson wanted to know where he had procured Mary's corpse. Burke changed his story, replying vaguely that he had purchased it from friends of the deceased. When Paterson queried him again about where her relatives lived, Burke looked at him suspiciously and said, according to the trial report: 'If I am to be catechised by you, where and how I get subjects, I will inform the doctor of it and if he allows you to do so I will bring no more to him, mind you.' Paterson had to accept Burke's story. Had he, Fergusson or any of the more perceptive students taken their suspicions to the police, the lives of Burke and Hare's future victims might have been spared.

Whatever its origins, it is clear that Mary Paterson's corpse made a dramatic impression on all who saw it. According to Burke's *Courant* confession (similar to his official confession but striking a more sensational note for the benefit of the general public), Knox was equally impressed by the naked but lifeless figure and brought in a painter to look at her. Burke added that 'she was not dissected at that time for she was three months in whisky before she was dissected'. Presumably this information came from David Paterson, who also stated that it was a common opinion among Knox's students and assistants that Mary's was a finely proportioned body, and that many of them took sketches of it. There is a definite whiff of necrophilia about all this. Mary survives in the Venus-like drawing by J. Oliphant (see plate 16), and it is a little macabre that the woman so admired was a lifeless corpse at the time.

Meanwhile the indefatigable Janet Brown and the lodging house madams continued to enquire as to Mary Paterson's whereabouts. Constantine Burke and his wife alleged that she had gone off to Glasgow with a packman, but although Mary was a girl of education and much attached to her friends, no letter came to relieve their anxiety, and her belongings remained unclaimed. Her disappearance was to remain a mystery until much later, when her clothes were discovered in the West Port house and produced at Burke's trial.

Had the disappearance occurred in Edinburgh's more orthodox circles or in the present century, her friends would of course have raised a hue and cry. Within 24 hours they would have reported the missing girl to the police and, considering that the body was not immediately dissected, there is a strong possibility that the crime would have been detected and the murderers apprehended. But those interested in Mary's fate belonged to a social class shy of the authorities. They had too much to hide in their own lives.

Janet continued her frantic search, scouring the streets for Mary. Meeting Constantine Burke one day, she tackled him for news of her friend and received a typical reply, as quoted by William Roughead in *Burke and Hare: Notable British Trials*:

'How the hell can I tell you about your sort of folk. You are here today and away tomorrow,' he said, adding that he could not answer for everything that took place in his house while he was out at work. A somewhat sinister remark in the circumstances, implying that he was aware that his wife was also implicated in the plot.

BUSINESS AS USUAL

Meanwhile Burke and Hare were back in business, lurking in the dark and dingy streets to pounce on likely 'subjects'. The destitute, feeble and homeless were their most vulnerable prey; creatures who depended on the kindness of strangers for a drink and a bed for the night. Their next victim a few weeks later in May 1828 was a destitute old woman who came to Hare looking for a night's lodging. She was plied with drink according to their usual methods and Burke suffocated her while Hare was out—although in his *Courant* confession he alleged that she had fallen asleep after being lured into the house by Hare's wife and that Hare had killed her. But Burke was sometimes contradictory and confused in his confessions. When he told this story he had been in the condemned cell for nearly three weeks and had every reason to implicate Hare as deeply as possible in the murders.

The next temporary lodger was a woman named Mary Haldane. According to Burke she was a stout old unmarried prostitute with only one large tooth in her mouth. She had two daughters, one of whom had been in Calton gaol until sentenced the previous summer to 14 years' transportation. Haldane fell asleep in a drunken stupor on straw in Hare's stable and the two suffocated her there, keeping the body hidden in the stable overnight and taking it to Surgeon's Square next day.

By this time Burke and Hare had six murders to their credit and had settled into a familiar routine. They no longer used a pillow or cushion to smother their victims, having discovered a more effective method that relied on their bare hands: one of them clapped one hand over the victim's mouth and held the nostrils closed with the other, while his partner lay across the body. This method had the supreme advantage that it left no marks on the body, and 'when they kept the mouth and nose shut a very few minutes,' Burke said in his *Courant* confession:

> they [the victims] could make no resistance but would convulse and make a rumbling noise in their bellies for some time after they ceased crying and making resistance, they left them to die of themselves, but their bodies would often move afterwards, and for some time they would have long breathings before life went away.

All was not over regarding their last victim. Peggy Haldane was the other daughter of the woman they had just murdered. She came in search of her mother, was lured in by drink and consoling assurances, and while helpless was killed by Burke.

An old cinder gatherer named Effie was the next body for the tea chest. She was a regular visitor to Burke and sold him small pieces of leather for his cobbling that she came across when 'raking the buckets' (searching the bins). On the day of her death Burke decided to be more hospitable than usual and inveigled her into Hare's stable. Drink was offered and consumed and as soon as Effie was helpless Burke summoned Hare. Effie's death followed in a now predictable manner.

Soon after this Burke had an unexpected stroke of luck. He met a policeman dragging a drunk old woman to the West Port watch. Informed that she had been found sitting on a stair, Burke confessed to being shocked by this treatment of her and offered to see her safely home. And so the policeman, relieved to be rid of the task, unwittingly delivered another victim to her doom. A few hours later the woman occupied the usual tea chest and her rescuer was congratulating himself on having saved her from an encounter with the watch house and the law. Again, if someone—in this case the policeman—had been more perceptive, the crimes of Burke and Hare might have been brought to light and their subsequent victims spared.

The year rolled on. It was now June and Burke and Hare were confirmed and casual killers. One day Burke in his daily search for subjects met a frail drunken old man of promising aspect. At the kindly prospect of another dram he was happy to accompany his benefactor to Tanner's Close. However in the High Street a hale old Irishwoman with a lad about 12 years old approached to ask Burke for directions. Penniless and destitute, she had tramped from Glasgow in the hope of meeting Edinburgh friends who had offered to help her. Now she was hopelessly lost: could Burke kindly assist her in finding these friends? He answered that of course he could. And it so happened that he knew the exact whereabouts of the folk she wanted and would escort her there forthwith.

The drunken old man, now considered inferior prey, was told to clear off. Watching them leave he loudly bewailed the loss of a dram, but had he known the price involved he would cheerfully have renounced strong drink for the rest of his days.

At the murder house the woman was persuaded to rest and

refresh herself from the bottle. Informing her that he was off to bring her friends, Burke summoned Hare, who arrived in his usual genial manner. Matters moved smoothly and swiftly and their guest was soon lying dead in the bed in the little back room, while the boy was left with Mrs Hare and Mrs Burke.

Here was a problem indeed. The boy was their victim's grandson and had been dumb from birth, facts which did not move these human fiends. What was to be done with him? As he was incapable of speech a solution occurred, perhaps to one of the women who still had something approximating to a heart or a conscience: that they put him outside to 'wander'. This idea was greeted with alarm by the others. It might lead to awkward consequences, especially if the boy led others to the house where he had last seen his grandmother. So it was decided that the boy should share her fate, and this seemed a better and better idea as the boy grew frightened and tearful at his grandmother's continued absence.

The next morning Hare went out to find the means to carry two bodies to Surgeon's Square. In the back room where the grandmother lay apparently asleep, Burke took the boy on his knee and as he expressed it, 'broke the bairn's back'. This conjures up a horrifying picture, but it is more likely that the boy was smothered, because a back injury might provoke curiosity even in Surgeon's Square. Whatever method was used, the scene continued to weigh heavily on Burke's mind, and he was haunted by the recollection of the piteous expression he had seen in the boy's eyes. Afterwards, it took a bottle of whisky to enable him to get to sleep each night.

The well-travelled tea chest being too small for a double load, the two bodies were forced into an old herring barrel and Hare's horse and cart was used to convey it to Surgeon's Square. But when they reached the Mealmarket in the Cowgate, the horse stopped and despite Hare's blows and curses, would go no further. The crowd that gathered at the scene was ready with advice—the last thing the two killers wanted—so a porter with a barrow was summoned to convey the barrel the rest of the way.

A FALLING OUT

Back in Tanner's Close domestic relationships were difficult and Burke and Helen departed for Falkirk, perhaps to visit her abandoned children or some relatives. Burke remembered the date—24 June—as it was also the anniversary of the Battle of Bannockburn. The reason for this break is obscure, but is probably based on the discord between the two women. According to Burke in his *Courant* confession, Hare's wife, who loathed Helen, wished her to 'be converted into merchandise; they could not trust her, as she was a Scotch woman'. The diabolical plan was that after disposing of Helen by the usual procedure, Burke was to go to the country and write to Hare that his wife

1 Edinburgh's Canongate Tolbooth in the 1860s. The scene would have been
similar at the time of Burke and Hare.

2 *Left*: Hare's house in Tanner's Close, from a drawing made at the time of its demolition in 1902.

3 *Above*: Contemporary drawing of William Hare, who in 1828 turned King's Evidence against his partner in crime William Burke.

4 *Left*: Burke's house from the back court, from an etching by Walter Geikie. 'A' shows Burke's window and 'B' the back entrance where the bodies were brought out.

5 *Right*: Burke the murderer, drawn from life on the day before his execution, by his consent.

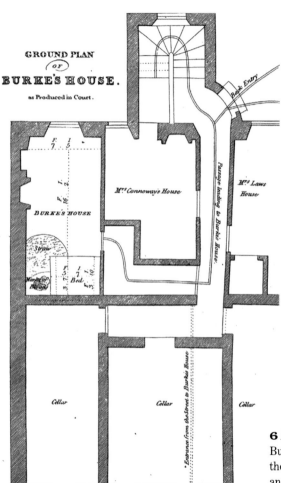

GROUND PLAN
OF
BURKE'S HOUSE.
as Produced in Court.

F. 1
7   5

F. 1
16. 2

BURKE'S HOUSE

Straw

Mrs Connoway's House

Passage leading to Burkes House.

Mrs Laws House

Back Entry

3. 7. Bed. £3. 10.
5. 7 1.

Cellar

Cellar

Cellar

Entrance from the Street to Burke House

PORTSBURGH

6 *Left*: Ground plan of
Burke's house, and
those of Mrs Connoway
and Mrs Law, who were
witnesses at his trial.

7 Interior of Burke's house, from a drawing by Charles Kirkpatrick Sharpe, showing at 2 'the straw under which the old woman [Mary Docherty] was hid'.

8 *Right*: Helen McDougal, the common-law wife of William Burke.

9 *Below*: Mrs Margaret (Maggie) Hare with babe in arms, as she appeared at Burke's trial.

10 *Far right*: Model of Dr Robert Knox in the History of Surgery Museum, Royal College of Surgeons, Edinburgh.

HELEN M'DOUGALL
THE ASSOCIATE OF WILLIAM BURKE
THE MURDERER

11 *Above*: Contemporary caricature of Dr Knox by one of his students.

12 *Right*: Poster advertising Dr Knox's lectures in 1828.

ANATOMY
AND
Physiology.

DR KNOX, F.R.S.E. *(Successor to* DR BARCLAY, *Fellow of the Royal College of Surgeons and Conservator of its Museum,)* will commence his ANNUAL COURSE or LECTURES ON THE ANATOMY AND **PHYSIOLOGY** of the Human Body, on Tuesday, the 4th November, at Eleven A. M. His Evening COURSE of LECTURES, on the same Subject, will commence on the 11th November, at Six P. M.

Each of these Courses will as usual comprise a full Demonstration on fresh Anatomical Subjects, of the Structure of the Human Body, and a History of the Uses of its various Parts; and the Organs and Structures generally, will be described with a constant reference to Practical Medicine and Surgery.

FEE for the First Course, £3, 5s.; Second Course, £2, 4s.; Perpetual, £5, 9s.

N. B.—These Courses of Lectures qualify for Examination before the various Colleges and Boards.

PRACTICAL ANATOMY
AND
OPERATIVE SURGERY.

DR KNOX'S ROOMS FOR **PRACTICAL ANATOMY** AND **OPERATIVE SURGERY**, will open on Monday, the 6th of October, and continue open until the End of July 1829.

Two DEMONSTRATIONS will be delivered daily to the Gentlemen attending the Rooms for PRACTICAL ANATOMY. These Demonstrations will be arranged so as to comprise complete Courses of the DESCRIPTIVE ANATOMY of the Human Body, with its application to PATHOLOGY and OPERATIVE SURGERY. The Dissections and Operations to be under the immediate superintendance of DR KNOX. Arrangements have been made to secure as usual an ample supply of Anatomical Subjects.

FEE for the First Course, £3, 5s.; Second Course, £2, 4s.; Perpetual, £5, 9s.

N. B.—*An Additional Fee of Three Guineas includes Subjects.*

❉ *Certificates of Attendance on these Courses qualify for Examination before the Royal College of Surgeons, the Army and Navy Medical Boards, &c.*

EDINBURGH, S   OR
        th Septe   ER,

Dr. Knox's Lectures, 1828.
in Original in the University of Edinburgh.

had died suddenly of a fever and had been buried at Falkirk. Hare would then show this letter to the neighbours to satisfy their curiosity. But Burke would not agree.

Before Burke and Helen left for Falkirk, Hare had been so short of funds that he pawned his clothes. On their return, however, Hare had plenty of money. Burke became suspicious that his partner had been doing business on his own account; this was hotly denied, but a visit to Surgeon's Square confirmed that Hare had supplied a woman's body for the price of £8.

Despite their agreed procedure, not one penny from this sale had come Burke's way. After a violent quarrel during which blows were exchanged, the two couples parted. Burke and Helen moved to the home of John Broggan, a carter whose wife was Burke's cousin. Their new lodging was in a five storey tenement two streets away from Tanner's Close. There was waste ground behind it, and Broggan's apartment was reached via a narrow passage from the West Port and down a flight of stone steps (see plate 4).

However, Burke and Hare needed each other and their inability to carry on their evil trade independently soon became apparent. Perhaps it was the fortuitous visit of Ann McDougal, a cousin of Helen's ex-partner, which cemented their reunion. Ann had come from Falkirk to visit her Edinburgh kinsfolk, doubtless on the strength of an invitation from the Burkes during their holiday. Genial hospitality in the form of drinking to insensibility speedily followed, but as Burke notes in his *Courant* confession, he found himself beset by scruples: 'As she being a distant friend, he did not like to begin first on her'. So Hare did the stifling and David Paterson provided 'a fine trunk to put her into'.

It was afternoon when Broggan came home from work. He remarked upon the new trunk and the absence of the country cousin. A few drams and a payment by each partner of £1 10s, as he was in arrears with his rent, was accepted as sufficient explanation. They gave him the money 'that he might not come against them for the murder of Ann McDougal, that he saw in the trunk, that was murdered in his house'.

The implication is that the two were either very drunk or very stupid and left the trunk open. But Broggan must have been suspicious, and prudently decided to leave the city immediately. He went off with his rent unpaid but with Ann's corpse sold for £10 as financial compensation.

Before Broggan left and Burke became sole occupier of his house, a charwoman called Mrs Hostler (or Ostler) became an irresistible target. She had 9½d in her hand and they could scarcely get it out after she was dead, so hard was it grasped. She was Burke and Hare's fourteenth victim.

CHAPTER THREE

Murder Will Out

===

If their luck had held Burke and Hare might have continued undetected for years. Usually killers are apprehended after the discovery of a corpse; dead bodies are notoriously hard to conceal indefinitely. But Burke and Hare had the perfect way of disposing of their victims' bodies, which were eagerly awaited (with no questions asked) for the dissecting tables at Surgeon's Square. Success however bred complacency, and the pair made two major mistakes that October. The first was Daft Jamie.

DAFT JAMIE

James Wilson was 18 years old (see plate 13). As his nickname implies, he was mentally subnormal, but was well known and loved on the streets of Edinburgh because of his inoffensive nature. His father had died when he was 12 and his mother supported them both by hawking cheap articles about the city.

One summer day Jamie wandered off with some local boys. When he failed to return, his mother, alarmed for his safety, shut up the house to go in search of him. In her absence he came home tired and hungry, burst open the door, and in his quest for food pulled down a cupboard, smashing all the household crockery. When his mother returned she was furious at this damage to her few precious possessions. She took a leather strap and thrashed him so vigorously that he left home, refusing to live with her again.

Jamie now wandered the streets in bare feet. Though physically big and strong for his years, he was partly paralysed on his right side and his feet were deformed, causing him to limp. He refused to wear shoes and to exchange his rags for the clothes offered by well-wishers, on the grounds that if people thought he was sufficiently well dressed they would no longer give him anything. Although he saw his mother regularly and she washed his clothes, he refused to stay in her house despite her pleas, spending his nights on stairs and in doorways unless some kindly soul offered him shelter.

Among his few possessions were a brass snuffbox and a copper spoon with seven holes, which he called after the days of the week, identifying the large one in the middle as Sunday. One of his favourite pastimes was asking riddles, but he would become very upset if the other person knew or guessed the answers. One unhappy morning this simple boy's path crossed that of killers in search of prey.

Burke was having a drink in Rymer's grog shop when he saw Maggie Hare taking Jamie Wilson across the street. A few minutes later she came in, bought a pennyworth of butter and asked Burke for a dram. While she was drinking it she stamped lightly on his foot (the first positive evidence of her complicity in the murders). Understanding her signal, Burke followed her back to Tanner's Close.

Hare was already there with Jamie and had provided him with the usual hospitable whisky. The two men then lured Jamie into the small room which had formerly been the Burkes' lodging. There, genial and smiling, they sat him on the bed and pressed him to have more whisky. Jamie was reluctant to do so, being 'very anxious and making enquiries for his mother', but was told that she would be there presently.

Maggie Hare then left the room and locked the three men inside, slipping the key under the door. As Burke said in his *Courant* confession (the source of the quotations here), 'she had led poor Jamie as a dumb lamb to the slaughter'. After a time, bemused and sleepy although not yet drunk, Jamie lay down on the bed. According to Burke, Hare reclined behind or beside him with his head resting on one hand, watching and awaiting an opportunity. Then, suddenly growing impatient, he 'threw his body on top of Jamie, pressed his hand on his mouth and held his nose with the other'.

Jamie put up a fierce fight, struggling so desperately that he and Hare fell off the bed. Hare hung on and Burke threw himself across Jamie's arms and legs, sustaining a painful injury to his testicles. Regardless, the two held on to their prey, while taking care not to leave signs of violence on his body. Overwhelming the boy took patience, but at last he ceased to struggle, went limp and died.

It was not yet noon when they stripped Jamie naked. Hare went through his pockets, kept the snuffbox and gave the spoon to Burke. Usually they took care to destroy their victims' clothing, but this time Burke gave Jamie's clothes to his brother Constantine for his children. In another break with routine, on receiving payment for the corpse Burke refused to pay Maggie £1 from his share, reasoning that he was not obliged to do so now he was no longer a tenant of Hare's. Maggie was so offended, having delivered Jamie into their hands, that she refused to speak to him for three weeks.

They put Jamie's body into Hare's clothes chest and carried it to Surgeon's Square. There the corpse was unpacked—and was immediately recognized as Daft Jamie by several of Knox's students. Jamie had been living in the house of James Downie, a porter at Stevenlaw's Close in the High Street, and it is hardly surprising that he should be known by sight. Knox's three assistants lived in the Old Town and almost everybody in that area as well as in the centre of Edinburgh must have been familiar with this innocent youth begging in the streets, a figure of fun to the insensitive and an object of compassion to others.

Of course, it is possible that Robert Knox, who operated on a different social plane, did not know Jamie—but what was he to do when he realized he had on his table the unburied corpse of a well-known character who had only recently been seen alive and well? By now Burke and Hare must have been regarded as invaluable contacts. Whatever suspicions crossed the minds of the doctor or his students, regular and reliable suppliers were not to be discouraged by awkward questions or any hesitation in paying the agreed price. According to Paterson, Knox denied that the corpse was that of Jamie; later, when word got around that Jamie had been missed from his customary haunts, Knox ordered his students to sharpen up their scalpels, and William Fergusson promptly severed Jamie's head and feet.

Did Paterson invent this account of the disposal of Jamie's corpse? By the time he made these damaging allegations in *Echoes of Surgeon's Square*, he had been sacked by Knox, and it is commonly believed that he wanted to avenge himself on his former employer. It was later rumoured that Paterson had been planning to go into partnership with Burke, travel to Ireland, procure more bodies, and despatch them to Hare who would sell them to Knox. This seems a very unlikely story, however. Burke had good reason not to trust Hare with money, and the illiterate Hare was the last man to be left in charge of public relations with the educated gentlemen of Surgeon's Square.

As for Jamie, this act of killing a well-known local character indicates Burke and Hare's now reckless belief that they were unstoppable. But it was the start of their undoing. None of their brutal murders was to cause more widespread horror than the killing of Jamie. When it became known there was a great public outcry, and a rash of sentimental ballads and broad-sheets were published (see plate 18).

THE LAST VICTIM

Halloween was regarded in Scotland at that time as the most perilous night of the year: folk believed in ghosts, witches, war-locks and devils, and saw them on every windy corner of Edin-burgh. But none was as devilish as Burke, who on the night of Friday 31 October in Rymer's grog shop met a poor Irish-woman named Mary Docherty begging for charity.

Burke heard the familiar accent, and when she told him she was from Inishowen in Donegal saw the perfect conditions for another 'shot': an old woman, destitute, frail, friendless, and with whom he could claim a fake connection. Burke turned on all his charm. 'Sure now, there's a coincidence,' he said, buying her a dram. 'If that wasn't my sainted mother's name, God rest her. And her an Inishowen woman too. We must be related!' Mary Docherty must have sighed with relief and thanked God that she had found a friend—and possibly a distant cousin— in this strange and frightening city. She told him she had come all the way from Glasgow to look for her son. Penniless and hungry, she had not eaten that morning. Burke said merrily that he could soon change all that. She was to come home with him and they would have some porridge and another dram to celebrate their meeting. Mary Docherty decided fatefully to accept.

At his lodging neighbours Mrs Connoway and Mrs Law, who were sitting at the fireside, saw them arrive through the open door. There were four others present in the house that day: Helen Burke, an ex-soldier named James Gray, his wife Ann, and their small child. Ann's maiden name was McDougal (her father was the father of Helen's two abandoned children), and she was no doubt distantly related to the Ann McDougal murdered by Burke and Hare.

Genial introductions made, Burke left Mrs Docherty with her new acquaintances, explaining that he was off to buy drink for the Halloween party that night. Instead he went to fetch Hare from Rymer's shop. After a whisper from Burke that he had 'a good shot for the doctors', Hare left immediately to inspect the merchandise. He found the old woman grateful for the kindness she had been offered by her kinsman. She was busy washing her shift, presumably in readiness for the celebrations that evening.

Burke and Hare decided that they had to get Burke's fellow lodgers, the Grays, off the premises. So Burke said to the Grays that as Mrs Docherty was a relation whom he had invited to stay, their bed would be required that night. Apologizing profusely for the inconvenience, he offered to pay for another bed for them: Maggie would escort them to Hare's lodging house in Tanner's Close.

Burke then left, this time genuinely to buy more drink. At

four in the afternoon, John Broggan, their ex-landlord's son—who called Mrs Burke 'auntie'—called in and met Mrs Docherty. When dusk descended Helen Burke called on Mrs Connoway, their neighbour across the passage. Explaining that she had to go out for a while, she asked Mrs Connoway to keep an eye on her door, which she said did not lock.

Some time later, Mr Connoway thought he heard someone go into the Burkes' lodging. Mrs Connoway took a light and went to investigate. Mrs Docherty was there alone, somewhat the worse for drink. She followed Mrs Connoway out, saying that she was going to meet someone in St Mary's Wynd who had promised to 'fetch her word about her son'. Mrs Connoway tried to dissuade her: it was dark outside and easy for a stranger—especially an inebriated one—to get lost in the maze of alleys. She might be picked up by the police and put in the watch house for the night. So Mrs Docherty went into Mrs Connoway's lodging for half an hour and retold her sad life story, stressing the wonderful coincidence of meeting a kinsman whose name was also Docherty. Mrs Connoway insisted that the man's name was actually Burke, but Mrs Docherty refused to believe that he had lied to her and went back to her lodging. Burke and Hare, who had now returned, were naturally relieved to see her again.

The whisky bottle made its round and by nine o'clock, when the Grays came back to collect their child's clothes, the party was in full swing. They saw Burke and Hare in merry mood drinking with their two womenfolk and Mrs Docherty, who was hale and hearty, accompanying Burke in singing the sentimental ballads of their native land. She also joined in the dancing in her bare feet and had her toe hurt jigging with Burke in his clumsy boots. To any observer, she was having a splendid time, and did not fit her label of 'old, frail and friendless'. (Later evidence suggests that she was between 40 and 50 and in good health: apart from a slight disorder of the liver, her internal organs were unusually sound with no signs of disease.)

Between 10 and 11 pm there was a general exodus of party-goers who had to rise early for work in the morning. However, according to the Connoways, the noisy party continued, until the sounds of revelry that kept them awake changed dramatically into less agreeable sounds. They heard the voices of Burke and Hare raised in anger, followed by scuffling sounds that indicated a fight—a typical end to festive occasions among the Irish community.

Between 11 pm and midnight, Hugh Alston, a grocer who lived above the shop that fronted the building, returned home to hear a noisy quarrel issuing from Burke's house and a woman's voice calling: 'Murder! For God's sake, someone—get the police.' Alarmed, Alston went in search of a policeman, but without success. When he came back all was quiet.

At about midnight, David Paterson, Dr Knox's doorkeeper, arrived home to find Burke hammering on his door. He was unsteady on his feet and urged Paterson to come back with him to his house. There Paterson found the Hares and Mrs Burke sitting drinking in the debris of the Halloween party. Wondering why he had been invited, Paterson was told that they had 'procured something for the doctor'. Burke pointed to the straw at one end of the bed and asked, could they have something on account? Paterson, doubtless feeling a little aggrieved at being dragged out at this time of night with such a request, told them smartly that only Dr Knox could authorize payment. They would have to wait.

Next morning, Mrs Burke went to Mrs Law to borrow bellows to get a fire started. When Mrs Law, who must have heard the altercations in the night, asked about Burke's kinswoman, Helen flew into a fury. She said that Mrs Docherty had been too free with William and that she 'had kicked the damned bitch's backside out of the door'. Mrs Law was relating this piece of gossip to Mrs Connoway when they were interrupted by a strange woman at the door asking if this was where Burke lived. This was David Paterson's sister, sent to fetch Burke; directed across the passage, she found Burke and took him to Paterson, who said that if Burke had anything to say or do with Dr Knox, he was to speak to him direct.

Burke returned to Tanner's Close, where he invited the Grays to his lodging for breakfast. They expected to see Mrs Docherty there, given that she had occupied their bed the previous night, but when they asked about her, Helen repeated her story about Mrs Docherty's over-familiarity with her husband.

As they were talking, Burke sprang to his feet and began splashing whisky about the room. He threw some up towards the ceiling and sprinkled more on the bed and on the straw on the floor, as well as over his own chest. The visitors were somewhat taken aback by this odd behaviour: Burke explained that he wanted the bottle empty in order to get it refilled.

This may have been simply an excuse to leave, but perhaps a more likely reason is his fear of what Mrs Gray might discover. While he was talking, Mrs Gray, who was smoking her clay pipe, started searching the alcohol-doused straw at the foot of the bed for her child's missing stockings. Burke turned on her furiously and told her to stay away from there. Soon afterwards she went back towards the bed, under which potatoes were kept. Again Burke intercepted angrily, demanding to know what she was doing near straw with a lighted pipe.

Burke went out, saying that he needed to buy more liquor, though his real mission was an urgent call at Surgeon's Square. There was still much activity at his house that afternoon, with neighbours drifting in and out. It was not until dusk that the Grays were alone and Mrs Gray was able to satisfy her curiosity about Burke's strange behaviour. She lifted the straw at the foot of the bed and uncovered first an arm, then the naked body of a woman with blood on her face. She and her husband immediately recognized the body as that of Mary Docherty.

Horrified, the Grays packed their belongings to leave, but Mrs Burke returned before they could do so. She asked why they were going in such a hurry, and Mr Gray answered that they had found a corpse in the house.

Realizing that the game was up, Helen Burke fell on her knees 'imploring that he would not inform of what he had seen'. Finding him quite unmoved, she offered a few shillings 'to put him over until Monday', adding that if they would hold their tongues, it would be worth £10 a week. Helen then appealed to Ann Gray, but was told, 'God forbid that my husband should be worth that for dead bodies.' When Ann remonstrated with Helen for bringing disgrace upon her family, Helen replied, 'My God, I cannot help it,' upon which Mrs Gray said sternly, 'You surely can help it or you would not stay in the house.'

Had it not been for the high-principled Grays—who were putting themselves at risk in owning to what they knew—Burke and Hare might have continued their murderous trade undetected. Refusing to be compromised or bribed, the Grays hurried away from Helen Burke, who followed, imploring them still. They encountered Maggie Hare who demanded to know what all the noise was about; when she was told what had happened she urged the Grays to return to the house to talk, instead of attracting attention by quarrelling in the street.

The Grays remained unmoved. Leaving the two women, they retired to a public house to consider what to do next. Mr Gray decided to go to the police while his wife went to Mrs Connoway and told her the whole horrifying story. Wanting a witness to their terrible discovery, she took Mrs Connoway into

Burke's house to view the body, but Mrs Connoway lost her nerve and returned home.

Meanwhile Burke was at Rymer's shop buying a tea chest which he said would be collected and paid for by Mrs Hare. At about six that evening, Burke offered a job to porter John McCulloch. Taken to Burke's house, McCulloch was shown the tea chest. Hare was present and the porter watched Burke put the body, together with some straw, into the chest. He noticed hair hanging out and stuffed it in before the lid was closed, the latter task requiring some pressure. McCulloch was then instructed to carry the chest along the Cowgate to the head of the High School Wynd, where Burke and Hare and their women caught up with him and led the way to Surgeon's Square.

Paterson was expecting the package and put it in the cellar. McCulloch was then asked by Burke to accompany them all—including Paterson and Mr Wharton Jones—to Dr Knox's house at 4 Newington Place, where Paterson and Jones went inside and told the doctor about the delivery. Knox handed over £5 on account, promising to supply the rest of the fee on sight of the body. At a nearby public house Paterson gave £2 10s each to Burke and Hare and 5s to the porter.

When Burke returned home he was met by Mr Connoway, who was eager to impart the sensational local gossip: that Burke had murdered his Halloween lodger. At that Burke laughed and, obviously still feeling infallible, said he did not care what all Scotland said about him.

MURDER, THEY SAID

As the tea chest was being delivered at Surgeon's Square, James Gray was at the police office reporting his suspicions to Sergeant John Fisher. The sergeant accompanied Gray and an officer named Findlay to Burke's house, where they found the Burkes on the stairs and about to leave again. Sergeant Fisher asked them to go back inside. The room was empty and, unsurprisingly, there was no body there. When Fisher asked what had become of his lodger, Burke pointed to Gray and said: 'There's one of them,' adding darkly that he had evicted the Grays the night before because of their bad conduct.

This put Fisher in something of a quandary. Was he on a wild goose chase? He knew the unsavoury characters of Tanner's Close: it was possible that the Grays had invented the whole story to get back at Burke. He asked Burke what had happened to the old woman who had been there the day before, to which Burke smoothly replied that she had left at about seven that morning and that Hare would be able to confirm this.

Fisher was now having doubts. Having taken a dislike to Burke's manner, he decided to take a look round the house. Examining the bed, he found bloodstains. Helen Burke said they had come from a previous female lodger having her period. For good measure she added that that evening in the Vennel, near the West Port, she had met Mrs Docherty, who had apologized for her conduct at the Halloween party.

Fisher then asked what time Mrs Docherty had left the house and was told seven on the Friday night. This raised a discrepancy between Burke's answer and his wife's, so Sergeant Fisher decided to take them both to the police office. There they were interviewed by a Lieutenant Paterson (no relation to David or Mary), who took the matter seriously and decided to investigate. That evening he and Fisher returned to Burke's house, accompanied by a police surgeon, Mr Alexander Black. They found signs of fresh blood on the straw and took away a striped nightgown which was lying on the bed.

At about seven in the morning on Sunday 2 November, the same two policemen, on the vague excuse of information received, paid David Paterson a visit at his home. He went with them to Dr Knox's premises at Surgeon's Square, where he unlocked the cellar and showed them the tea chest still tied with rope. The box was opened and the naked corpse of a woman found doubled up inside; its face was a livid colour and there was blood round the mouth.

Mr Gray was sent for. He identified the body as that of Mrs Docherty, whom he had seen and heard at Burke's house on Friday night, and as the corpse he and his wife had seen dead under the straw next morning. The body was removed to the police office, where Mrs Law and Mrs Connoway confirmed the identification. The police surgeon, Mr Black, examined the corpse, concluding that the woman had probably died by violence, but that he could not say so with certainty.

Instructions were issued for the arrest of the Burkes and the Hares (see plate 14). Arriving at Tanner's Close early that morning, the police found the Hares still in bed; they were informed that Lieutenant Paterson wished to have a word with them about a dead body found in Burke's house. Maggie Hare responded indignantly that surely the police had better things to do than waste their time over a drunken spree. Hare then said that as he had been in Burke's house the night before having a drink, and might be blamed, he had better rise and see what was wrong. The Hares were arrested, taken to the police office and like the Burkes lodged in separate cells. When the four were confronted with the corpse of their last victim, in typical fashion they denied everything. All stated volubly that they had never seen this woman before, alive or dead.

Meanwhile the press had got hold of the news and rumour spread through the city. The *Edinburgh Evening Courant* of 3 November 1828 reported the case in grim detail.

THE BURKES TELL ALL

The details given of the murders committed by Burke and Hare are drawn from Burke's two confessions and from evidence given by witnesses at the trial. Hare's initial statement concerning the events leading to Mrs Docherty's death has been lost to posterity, but whatever its content it could not have been more fantastic than that first given by Burke. He said that on the evening of Friday 31 October (after he had dismissed the Grays because he could not support them any longer), an anonymous stranger in a greatcoat with a cape concealing his face had called to have a pair of shoes mended. While Burke did this, the man remarked that this was a quiet place and asked if he might leave a box there to collect shortly.

Burke readily agreed and the man departed, returning shortly with a box which he unroped beside the bed, making a rustling noise in the straw. Burke was too intent on making a good job of his honest toil to take much notice of what he was doing. The stranger paid 6d for the repairs and left, after which Burke, curious about the contents of the box, opened it and found it empty. But the villainous stranger had concealed a dead body under the straw alongside the bed. Whether the corpse was male or female, Burke did not find out before the man's return. Challenged by Burke, he agreed to remove the box and its contents, but said he could not do so until the next night, which was Saturday.

Burke then paused to mention his meeting with Mrs Docherty in Rymer's shop that Saturday morning. She left his house at 3 pm: his wife, Mrs Hare and Mrs Connoway had all witnessed her departure. She never returned but at 6 pm the stranger reappeared, accompanied by a porter whom Burke knew by sight and whose Christian name he believed to be John. This was in fact John McCulloch. The stranger agreed to pay Burke two guineas for safeguarding the box and mentioned that the dead body was destined for Surgeon's Square. Burke suggested that he consult David Paterson, who he believed had some connection with the surgeons, and the two of them set off for that address. There Paterson handed the stranger some amount—Burke did not know how much exactly—and the stranger gave him £2 10s for his trouble.

Burke then said that the dead body shown to him at the police office bore no resemblance to Mrs Docherty, who was not nearly so tall. Questioned by the Sheriff, he said he now believed the stranger to be none other than William Hare, with whom he admitted some previous acquaintance. He continued to deny that Mrs Docherty had set foot in his house on the Friday and that he had set eyes on her before the Saturday. He had no idea what had become of her since then.

Mrs Burke was then interrogated. Her account was less colourful than Burke's, and it was also completely contradictory. She stated that while they were at breakfast on the fatal Friday, an old woman the worse for liquor came in and asked if she could light her pipe at the fire. As it transpired that she was a relative of Burke's mother, she was hospitably received and they had a glass all round, this being the custom of Irish people at Halloween.

Later in the day, their guest seemed anxious to go to St Mary's Wynd to enquire after her son, and she left at 2 pm. Meanwhile it was arranged that the Grays should take a room in Tanner's Close, Mrs Connoway having complained about the noise of their quarrels. The Hares spent Halloween night with the Burkes and there was a lot of drinking. Next morning, the Grays came back to breakfast and in the afternoon, Mrs Gray, accused of stealing one of Helen Burke's gowns, 'raised a disturbance'. She and her husband then went to the police office with a complaint, and that was when the two officers came back and made their arrests.

Mrs Burke concluded her statement by declaring emphatically that she had never seen the old woman after Friday (a direct contradiction to her initial story of meeting with Mrs Docherty in the Vennel) and that the dead body was definitely not that of Mrs Docherty; the latter's hair was dark, whereas that of the corpse was grey. She went on to say that she had known nothing of a body concealed in the house until the arrest of herself and her husband. She denied having any conversation with the Grays regarding a body or trying to bribe Gray to hold his tongue.

Meanwhile, the post-mortem examination had been conducted by Professor Robert Christison. He concluded that there was justification for suspicion of death by suffocation, such as strangling, smothering or throttling, but that this could not be proved by medical science. Following the post-mortem, Burke, Hare and the two women were brought before Sheriff-substitute Mr George Tait and the Procurator Fiscal, Mr Archibald Scott. The charge was murder.

CHAPTER FOUR

Trial and Execution

On 6 November the *Edinburgh Evening Courant* published its report of the initial statements made by Burke, Hare and their wives. The parties arrested, it said, had given very contradictory accounts of the manner in which the old woman lost her life: 'one of the men, not Burke, states that it was the lad Broggan who struck her in the passage and killed her. Burke, however, acknowledges being a party to the disposing of the corpse.' The report ended by saying that 'the above are the outlines of the statements that have reached us. We must, however, admit that, from the secret manner in which the investigations are conducted, it is impossible to obtain accurate confirmation.'

On 10 November the Burkes were again brought before the Sheriff. This time Burke changed his story. He admitted that he had been mistaken about the dates: it was on the Friday, not the Saturday, that the old woman had come to his house, and she had in fact been present at the Halloween party where the drink flowed 'till they were pretty hearty'. In the course of the night he and Hare had fallen out, fought, and afterwards missed the woman. Presuming she had left, they then found her seemingly drunk and unconscious, lying against the wall at the foot of the bed. She had ceased to breathe. When they saw she was dead, Hare suggested they strip the body and sell it to the surgeons.

Burke denied that he had seen Paterson about delivery of the body on the Friday night before the party. When the Sheriff asked him whether the body at the police office was that of the woman in question, he replied that he could not say, but that no harm had been done by anyone to the old woman who was at his house. She was suffocated, he believed, 'by laying herself down among the straw while in a state of intoxication'. And although no violence was shown to her in life, 'a good deal of force was necessary to get the body into the chest, as it was stiff and some injuries may have been caused'. He added that young John Broggan knew nothing of the transaction.

Helen Burke adhered to her former statement, except to say that as the old woman became 'very troublesome' between 3 and 4 pm on Friday afternoon, she thrust her out the door by the shoulders and never saw her afterwards. She added that Burke and Hare had had a slight difference on the Friday night, but that no great noise had been made and no cries of murder as far as she heard.

Young Broggan, who had been arrested on suspicion of involvement in the murder, was released, the police being satisfied of his innocence. The Burkes and Hares were held in Calton gaol, arraigned for the murder of Mrs Docherty, while an anxious public, relieved to know that the murderers were safely behind bars, eagerly waited to hear the date for a trial which promised to be the most sensational in Edinburgh's legal history.

THE LAW'S DILEMMA

Meanwhile the Lord Advocate, Sir William Rae, was faced with a dilemma. The primary task of the Public Prosecutor was the establishment of what in Scots law is termed the *corpus delictii*: the fact that murder has been committed. But Burke and Hare's methods were subtle: smothering left little evidence of violence. As a result, the post-mortem examination of Mrs Docherty, the only corpse at the disposal of the police surgeons, had been much less conclusive than hoped. The newspapers were quick to publicize the fact that the medical establishment had not confirmed so far that the old woman died by violence.

Mr Alexander Black, surgeon to the Edinburgh City Police, had first examined the body, commenting only on various contusions on the upper lip, back and scapula, none of which were of a nature to cause immediate death. His private opinion, stated afterwards, was that the woman had died from violence, but medically he could not confirm that this was the cause of death. Other medical men were also hesitant about saying with any certainty that Mrs Docherty had been murdered.

DAFT JAMIE.

From an Original Drawing.—1829

13 Contemporary drawing of Daft Jamie with his characteristic rags and bare feet.

Unto The Hon'ble The Sheriff
of Edinburghshire

The Petition of Archibald Scott
Procurator Fiscal of Court for
the Public interest

Humbly Sheweth

That on Sunday last the Thirty
first of October last Mysie or Madgy
McGonnegaI or Campbell or Duffy
from Ireland & then residing in
Edinburgh was seen in the house
of William Burke a Shoemaker
in Wester Portsburgh near Edinburgh
in good health and on the following
day her body was seen lifeless
under a bed in said House and
afterwards it was discovered that it
had been sold to a Lecturer on
Anatomy That from information re-

WILLIAM BURKE and HELEN M'DOUGAL, both present prisoners in the tolbooth of Edinburgh, you are both and each of you Indicted and Accused at the instance of Sir WILLIAM RAE of St Catharines, Baronet, his Majesty's Advocate, for his Majesty's interest: THAT ALBEIT, by the laws of this and of every other well governed realm, MURDER is a crime of an heinous nature, and severely punishable: YET TRUE IT IS AND OF VERITY, that you the said William Burke and Helen M'Dougal are, both and each, or one or other of you, guilty of the said crime, actors or actor, or art and part: IN SO FAR AS, on one or other of the days between the 7th and the 16th days of April 1828, or on one or other of the days of that month, or of March immediately preceding, or of May immediately following, within the house in Gibb's close, Canongate, Edinburgh, then and now or lately in the occupation of Constantine Burke, then and now or lately scavenger in the employment of the Edinburgh police establishment, you the said William Burke did wickedly and feloniously place or lay your body or person, or part thereof, over or upon the breast or person and face of Mary Paterson or Mitchell, then or recently before that time, or formerly, residing with Isabella Burnet or Worthington, then and now or lately residing in Leith street, in or near Edinburgh, when she the said Mary Paterson or Mitchell was lying in the said house in a state of intoxication, and did, by the pressure thereof, and by covering her mouth and nose with your body or person, and forcibly compressing her throat with your hands, and forcibly keeping her down, notwithstanding her resistance, or in some other way to the Prosecutor unknown, preventing her from breathing, suffocate or strangle her; and the said Mary Paterson or Mitchell was thus, by the said means, or part thereof, or by some other means or violence, the particulars of which are to the Prosecutor unknown, wickedly bereaved of life and murdered by you the said William Burke; and this you did with the wicked aforethought intent of disposing of, or selling the body of the said Mary Paterson or Mitchell, when so murdered, to a physician or surgeon, or some person in the employment of a physician or surgeon, as a subject for dissection, or with some other wicked and felonious intent or purpose to the Prosecutor unknown. (2.) FURTHER, on one or other of the days between the 5th and 26th days of October 1828, or on one or other of the days of that month, or of September

14 *Far left*: The petition for the arrest of the Burkes and Hares, 3 November 1828, in relation to the death of Madgy McGonnegal (Mary Docherty).

15 *Left*: First page of the indictment against the Burkes, describing Mary Paterson's murder.

16 *Below*: Drawing of Mary Paterson before dissection; her body was much admired by the medical students.

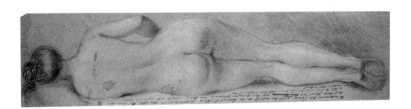

71

Murder

Sentence of Death
ag.t
Willm Burke

carried from the Bar back to the
Tolbooth of Edinburgh, therein to be
detained and to be fed upon bread
and water only in terms of an act
of Parliament passed in the twenty
fifth year of the reign of his Majesty King George the Second entitled
"An Act for preventing the horrid
crime of Murder" until Wednesday the twenty eighth day of
January next to come, and upon
that day to be taken furth of the
said Tolbooth to the common Place
of Execution in the Lawnmarket
of Edinburgh and then and there
between the hours of Eight and
Ten o'clock before noon of the
said day to be hanged by the
neck by the hands of the common Executioner upon a gibbet
until he be dead and his body
thereafter to be delivered to Doctor
Alexander Munro, Professor of
Anatomy in the University of
Edinburgh to be by him publicly dissected and anatomised in
terms of the said act and ordain
all his moveable goods and
gear to be escheat and inbrought
to his Majestys use which is pro-
nounced for doom.
              Signed D. Boyle
                     Alex Maconochie
                     J. H. Mackenzie

17 *Left*: Notes from Burke's trial recording his sentence, which included a bread and water diet in his condemned cell, hanging by the neck and public dissection by Dr Alexander Munro.

18 *Right*: Broadsides offering sentimental poetry and sensational accounts of the crimes were sold on Edinburgh street corners.

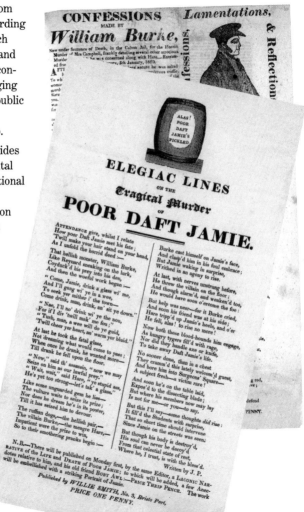

19 *Below*: The death mask of William Burke, in the History of Surgery Museum, Royal College of Surgeons, Edinburgh.

20 *Below*: A wallet made from Burke's skin after the dissection of his body, in the History of Surgery Museum, Royal College of Surgeons, Edinburgh.

21 *Above*: The frenzied
scene of Burke's execu-
tion on 28 January 1829.

quantities at different shops, there was no water or other
liquid put in the cup with the rum & Laudanum - the
Boy drank the contents of the Cup directly, in two draughts
& afterwards a little Beer - in about ten minutes he fell
asleep on the Chair on which he sat & I removed him from
the Chair to the Floor & laid him on his side - we then
went out and left him there - we had a quartern of gin
& Pint of Beer at the Feathers near Shoreditch Church &
then went home again having been away from the Boy
about 20 minutes we found him asleep as we had left
him - we took him directly, asleep & insensible, into the
Garden & tied a cord to his feet to enable us to pull
him up by it & I then took him in my arms & let him
slide from them headlong into the well in the Garden
whilst Williams held the cord to prevent his Body going
altogether too low into the well - he was nearly wholly
in the water of the well - his feet just above the surface
Williams fastened the other end of the cord round the
paling to prevent the Body getting beyond our reach
the Boy struggled a little with his arms & legs in the
water - & the water bubbled for a minute - we waited
till these symptoms were past & then went in doors &
afterwards I think we went out & walked down -
Shoreditch to occupy the time & in about 3 quarters
of an hour we returned & took him out of the well
by pulling him by the cord attached to his feet - we
undressed him in the paved Yard - rolled his Clothes up
& buried them where they were found by the witness who
produced them - we carried the Boy into the washhouse
laid him on the floor & covered him over with a Bag
we left him there & went & had some Coffee in Old Street
Road & then (a little before two in the morning of Friday
went back to my House - we immediately doubled the

22 *Left*: The 1831 confession of London 'burker' John Bishop, discovered in 2006 in the National Archives. It relates how John Bishop and Thomas Williams murdered the 'Italian Boy' after plying him with drink, and sold his body for dissection. Comparisons were made at the time with the Burke and Hare killings.
(HO 17/46)

Here was a legal quandary indeed. Although the police suspected that other murders had been committed, there were no bodies to substantiate this (multiple murder was confirmed only by Hare's evidence to the trial and Burke's later confessions). All they had to go on was one dead woman, an apparent motive, several witnesses and four suspects in prison who, although repeatedly examined, positively denied murder. With such flimsy information at its disposal, the prosecution could not count on a successful outcome. Even if it was established beyond reasonable doubt that the corpse in question had been murdered, the identity of the culprits would still be impossible to prove.

A month had passed since the four were apprehended and the Lord Advocate now knew that the evidence, including the medical report, was inconclusive. Aware that outside the courts lurked an anxious public, he saw the vital importance of securing an early conviction. He was reluctant, however, to try the suspects on inadequate evidence, no doubt bearing in mind the famous Scottish 'Not proven' verdict, which had allowed many criminals a narrow escape from the gallows. (This verdict was popularly interpreted as 'We know you did it. Go away and don't do it again!')

So Sir William decided that one of the four had to be persuaded to testify against the other three. On meeting Burke he had concluded that here was a literate man with some education, and that therefore he was the principal party in the affair. Furthermore, it would be possible for Helen Burke or McDougal to testify against him because they were not legally married. But Helen refused to give any information, and Maggie Hare could not legally testify against her husband. So the Lord Advocate, possibly encouraged by his readiness to implicate the boy Broggan in the murder, authorized an approach to Hare to turn King's Evidence. On 1 December Hare was offered immunity from prosecution if he would disclose the facts about Mrs Docherty's murder and any other such crimes committed by Burke. This was eagerly accepted, and Hare detailed the series of murders, laying all the blame on Burke. In doing so, Hare guaranteed Maggie's freedom, as he could not testify against his wife.

Consternation, anger and fear among Edinburgh citizens had already been reported in the press, which seized this rare chance to boost circulations by offering sensational and inaccurate revelations regarding the number of murder victims. Public disquiet was also stimulated by popular broadsheets on sale in the streets. The panic quickly spread beyond Edinburgh and police offices nationwide were besieged by relatives and friends of missing persons, all now assumed to be murder victims. Among the locals who learned of the arrest of Burke and Hare was Janet Brown, who was still concerned about the disappearance of her friend Mary Paterson. Now she guessed the terrible truth. Aware perhaps for the first time of her own narrow escape, she told the police all she knew, identifying the prisoners in whose company she had last seen Mary. In addition, a local shopkeeper claimed to have seen one of Constantine Burke's sons wearing a pair of trousers which he had given to Daft Jamie.

And so the net closed. The Local Advocate was now confident that a successful case could be brought against William Burke for the murders of Mary Paterson, James Wilson and Mrs Docherty, and against Burke's common law wife Helen for that of Mrs Docherty. Within days of Hare's betrayal, the Burkes were charged and committed for trial before the High Court of Justiciary.

THE TRIAL

The date set was 24 December 1828. If this seems an odd choice, it must be remembered that before Queen Victoria came to the throne and her consort Prince Albert introduced the Christmas tree from Germany, Christmas celebrations as we know them did not exist. In Georgian Scotland 24 December was just another winter's day.

A huge crowd had assembled to await the arrival of the accused from Calton gaol to the cells below the High Court. They had seen nothing like this since the banquet for King George IV in the magnificent Parliament Hall in 1822. However, this crowd was in a very different mood from the one gathered on that splendid occasion: inflamed by the terrible events in Tanner's Close, its members were there to see justice done and the murderers sentenced to death. Trouble was expected, and troops of cavalry and infantry were on standby; 300 extra constables had been drafted in to assist the local police, though this number proved hopelessly inadequate to deal with a potential riot when the mob found the approaches to the court closed to them. The courtroom had been packed to overflowing since it opened its doors at 9 am. Among those fortunate enough to get a seat was a lady who had come all the way from Paris: this was Madame Tussaud, who had come to add the notorious William Burke to her famous waxworks. The crowd surged into the Old Town's main thoroughfares, the Lawnmarket, the High Street and Cowgate, its anger not sweetened by a wait of several hours in freezing cold and rain.

In the stifling atmosphere inside the court, proceedings began with lengthy legal preliminaries. These were followed by the indictment (see plate 15): William Burke stood accused of the murder of Mary Paterson, James Wilson and Mary Docherty (or Campbell), Helen McDougal of only the last crime.

This was followed by a lengthy debate on relevancy between the prosecution, led by the Lord Advocate, and the defence, led by the Dean of the Faculty for Burke and Mr Henry Cockburn (later to become Lord Cockburn) for Helen McDougal. Burke's defence began by objecting to the accumulation of separate charges. This was the first case in which an attempt had been made by a prosecutor to charge, in one libel, three unconnected murders committed at different times. Not only was this inconsistent with the principles of Scottish law, but it would prejudice the minds of the jury.

It was midday on Christmas Eve when the trial proper began. Accompanied by an excited murmur and craning of necks, William Burke and Helen McDougal were placed at the bar. The *Caledonian Mercury* described them in its issue of 25 December 1828:

> The male prisoner is rather below the middle size, but stoutly made and of a determined, though not peculiarly sinister expression of countenance. A round face with high cheek bones, grey eyes a good deal sunk in the head, a short snubbish nose and a round chin. His hair and whiskers are of a light sandy colour, his complexion of nearly the same hue. He was dressed in a shabby blue surtout, buttoned close to the throat and had upon the whole, a less than ferocious expression, though there is a hardness about the features mixed with an expression in the grey eyes far from inviting.
>
> The female prisoner is fully of the middle size, but thin and spare made, though evidently of large bone. Her features are long and the upper half of her face is out of proportion to the lower. She was miserably dressed in a small grey-coloured velvet bonnet, very much the worse for the wear, a printed cotton shawl and cotton gown. She stoops considerably in her gait, and has nothing peculiar in her appearance, except the ordinary look of extreme poverty and misery common to unfortunate females of the same degraded class. Both prisoners,

especially Burke, entered the Court without any visible signs of
trepidation and both seemed to attend very closely to the proceedings which soon after commenced.

The couple were asked to answer only the third charge in the
indictment, that of murdering Mary Docherty. Both pleaded
not guilty.

The jury was sworn: 15 men from the upper echelons of middle-class Edinburgh, including merchants and artisans and the
bookseller Thomas Nelson. The portrait painter George Andrew
Lutener was present, although his name did not come out in the
ballot, and he made a drawing of Maggie Hare with her child in
her arms (see plate 9).

The list of 55 witnesses included Dr Knox and his three
assistants, Fergusson, Jones and Miller; also Janet Brown,
Constantine Burke and his two sons, Richard and William—but
none of these was called. Items produced as evidence included
clothing belonging to the three victims, a linen sheet and pillow-
case and a brass snuffbox and spoon (once the cherished possessions of Daft Jamie).

Among the first witnesses was builder James Braidwood,
who produced a plan of Burke's house (see plate 6), and Mary
Stewart, who testified that Mary Docherty had left her lodging
house on the morning of Friday 31 October in good health and
of a sober disposition; this was confirmed by fellow lodger
Charles McLauchlan. Both witnesses had identified the body.

Hugh Alston took the stand and confirmed that, returning

to his house late that night, he

> heard two men making a great noise, as if wrangling or quar-
> relling. I heard no strokes or blows—there was a woman's
> voice that attracted my particular attention, crying murder, but
> not in a way I considered her in imminent danger. But it was
> a very strong voice for a female, and standing there listening
> a minute or two, there was something gave a cry, as if from
> a person, or animal that had been strangled. The two men were
> making a lot of noise and she struck on something, slapping the
> door, as if crying for the police she cried 'murder here.' After
> this I went for a policeman but could not find one. When I
> returned I heard the men speaking and the woman had ceased
> to cry murder, so I thought everything was over.
> (From William Roughead's *Notable British Trials*)

Mrs Connoway and Mrs Law also gave their account of the noisy
Halloween party and confirmed that they had heard sounds of
fighting and struggling afterwards, which they took to be
between Burke and Hare.

David Paterson's appearance caused a stir in the court
because of his close association with Dr Knox. He told how
Burke had come to his house at midnight, drunk and unsteady
on his feet, and narrated the events the next day leading to the
dramatic opening of the tea chest in Knox's cellar. He described
the previous arrival of Burke and Hare with the tea chest,
claiming that this was one of many such visits, and that he paid
them on Knox's instructions.

Paterson was then asked if he knew of any dealings Dr Knox

had had with Burke before the business of the dead bodies, and replied in the affirmative. In fact, although this did not come out during the trial or in the newspapers, Burke had attended Knox to receive treatment 'for his wound'. Atlay's *Famous Trials of the Century* reveals that Burke was in fact suffering from advanced testicular cancer, which would have killed him had the hangman not got there first.

John McCulloch, the porter, now told the court how he had been summoned by Burke to convey the tea chest to Surgeon's Square, and had accompanied Burke and Hare and their women to Newington for payment.

Mrs Gray told of Burke's excuse for sending them to sleep at the Hares' on the party night, and to a hushed court described her discovery of the body of the murdered woman in the straw. This was confirmed by Mr Gray, who also described Helen Burke's futile attempts to pay them for their silence, and how he had gone to the police.

Sergeant John Fisher then took the stand and related the events of his visit to Burke's house. The body had disappeared by then, he said, but he identified an exhibit which was handed to him: the striped nightgown which had been lying on the bed. He told of his visit to Surgeon's Square and the production of the tea chest containing the naked corpse formally identified by Mrs Gray. The body had been shown to the prisoners who had denied having seen it before, dead or alive. Sergeant Fisher's evidence was to arouse adverse criticism in the 1 January edition of the *Caledonian Mercury*:

> It does not appear that the officers of police had the slightest
> intelligence of any one of the murders which are now known to
> have been committed, and but for the information given by the
> man Gray, the whole mystery might have still remained in full
> operation. The police had no merit whatever in this affair, and
> indeed its officers act upon a principle which actually affords
> facilities for the repetition of similar crimes. They have instruc-
> tions not to interfere in such scenes … unless they either see it,
> or some informant commits an offender to custody.

Outside the courtroom a clock struck six. The court had been in
session for nine hours, and still in the darkness and freezing
cold a crowd waited, some there since early morning.

The star witness was called. As Hare took the oath he was
warned that if he deviated from the truth in the slightest degree,
he would be liable to the death penalty. Did a tremor of revul-
sion run around the assembled court at his sinister appearance?
With his hollow cheeks and ghastly smile he must have looked
more like a murderer than Burke, whose appearance was
described by Lord Cockburn some years later in *Memorials of
His Time* as that of 'a respectable man not at all ferocious in his
general manner'. Certainly Hare made a less than favourable
impression, according to the 27 December edition of the
Caledonian Mercury:

> 'this squalid wretch' as Mr Cockburn so picturesquely called
> him, from the hue and look of the carrion crow in the witness

box, was disposed to be extremely communicative, and apparently had no idea that anything he had stated was at all remarkable or extraordinary. The conviction of Burke alone will not satisfy either the law or the country.

All went well with Hare's testimony until questions were raised on the supply of multiple bodies to the doctors in addition to the one in dispute. Hare was warned that he was not bound to answer questions which might incriminate himself, for in doing so he was not under the court's protection. In response to several of these questions he paused briefly and said 'Not to answer.'

Maggie Hare then took the stand, clutching her child, whose frequent paroxysms of whooping cough gave its mother useful time to consider her responses. Twice, somewhat confused, she took refuge in the excuse of a very bad memory. Confirming most of Hare's assertions, she said that 'the thing [the death of a woman] had happened two or three times before and it was not likely that I should tell a thing to affect my husband'. The implication was that she was afraid she might herself be murdered. She claimed to have left Hare three times because she was 'not leading a contented life'.

The final witnesses were Mr Alexander Black and Professor Christison. Their evidence was of little help to the prosecution, for although both agreed that there were strong grounds for suspicion, neither could say definitely that Mrs Docherty had died as a result of violence.

There were no witnesses for the defence. The two pre-trial

declarations of William and Helen Burke (see Chapter 3) were next read out. Then after a trial 'of unprecedented nature—of nearly unexampled duration' (it had lasted almost 23 hours), in the early hours of Christmas Day the jury was addressed at length by the Lord Advocate, the Dean of the Faculty and Mr Henry Cockburn. The judge concluded by instructing the jury to return such a verdict as justice required.

Meanwhile, throughout the long hours of the trial, the police had had to deal with various disturbances outside the court. A small crowd of youths set off for Dr Knox's house in Newington, and there were ugly scenes as the police with difficulty restrained them from damaging his property. Thwarted, the youths went to the university and worked off their frustrations by breaking windows in the anatomy lecture rooms.

DEATH BY HANGING

Awaiting the jury's reappearance, Burke sat apparently unmoved, while Helen was very agitated. After 50 minutes, the jury filed back. In a hushed silence their chairman, John McFie, addressed the court: 'The jury find William Burke guilty of the third charge in the Indictment, the murder of Mary Docherty and find the Indictment "not proven" against Helen McDougal.'

This verdict was followed by uproar in the court. As Helen wept, Burke clutched her hand and said, 'Nelly, you're out of the scrape.' Newspapermen fled to be first to break the news, as the Lord Justice-Clerk thanked the jury for a verdict that would appear to be perfectly well founded and for giving the female prisoner the benefit of their doubts. In fact, the jury's decision had not been unanimous—two of its members had favoured a 'not proven' verdict for Burke.

The judge donned the black cap. After expressing his doubts as to whether, in accordance with the law passed in 1752, Burke's body should hang in chains as a deterrent to those considering similar crimes in the future, he opted for the customary sentence of dissection after execution. He added that 'if it is ever customary to preserve skeletons yours will be preserved, in order that posterity may keep in remembrance your atrocious crimes'. (And so it remains to this day, an exhibit in the Museum at The Royal College of Surgeons along with a wallet made from Burke's skin; see plate 20.)

The formal sentence followed (see plate 17). Burke was to be taken back to the Tolbooth of Edinburgh and fed on bread and water only until Wednesday 28 January 1829, when he was to be taken to the common place of execution in the Lawnmarket and hanged by the neck until dead. Afterwards his body was to be delivered to Dr Monro to be publicly dissected and anatomized. Dismissing Helen McDougal the judge reminded her that she had not been declared not guilty; her own conscience must draw the proper conclusion.

The court rose as clocks across Edinburgh struck ten. The

trial had lasted 24 hours without any adjournment for rest or refreshment, and the *Caledonian Mercury* was already printing:

> No trial in the memory of any man now living has excited so
> deep, universal and (we may almost add) appalling an interest
> as that of William Burke and his female associate... [It is] the
> first instance of murder with the aforethought purpose and
> intent of selling the murdered body as a subject for dissection
> to Anatomists; it is a new species of assassination, or murder
> for hire and as such was certainly calculated to make a deep
> impression on the public mind.

For their own safety the Burkes were kept in the cells at Parliament House for the rest of the day. Hostile crowds filled the streets outside the court, besieging the newspaper offices for reports of the trial and incensed that only Burke had received the death penalty.

Early the next morning, the couple were removed to Calton gaol where Burke was put in the condemned cell. 'This is a bloody cold place you have brought me to!' he complained. Whatever dinners could be afforded by the exhausted officials and spectators of the court, Burke had only bread and water.

Mrs Burke was released that evening, and the two never met again. She went home and stayed indoors for most of the next day, but by evening the craving for whisky drove her out. She was greeted with an angry howl by crowds milling around the house, who had awaited just such an opportunity and fully intended to take the law into their own hands. The police arrived just before they could lynch her. Using their batons freely, they removed her to the safety of the West Portsburgh watch house, followed by the frustrated mob demanding vengeance and smashing windows. At last, dressed as a man, Mrs Burke was smuggled out to the police office in Liberton's Wynd for the night, while the police placated the angry crowd with the story that she was being held there to give evidence against Hare (who was still in prison with his wife Maggie for their own safety).

Before quitting Edinburgh in some haste, Helen Burke, along with Burke's brother Constantine, tried to visit the convicted man in gaol, but permission was refused. Mrs Burke spent a brief sojourn in Falkirk which came to an end when she was recognized. She fled to Newcastle, where she had no better luck. After being escorted to the Durham border, all trace of her was lost, although a rumour circulated long afterwards that she had reached Australia.

While Burke awaited death in the condemned cell, questions were being asked about the validity of the trial, which had in the view of the general public fallen far short of achieving justice for Burke and Hare's victims. There was more than a suggestion that mob violence would ultimately result, although the public at this point knew only of evidence for the murders of Mary Paterson and Daft Jamie and had no idea about the other killings; Burke had not yet given his confession to the *Courant* from gaol.

When the details of the trial were published, there was a general outcry against Dr Knox. Many felt that he ought to have been in the dock alongside his suppliers. Why had he not been called as a witness? The reason given was that he had never seen the body of Mary Docherty. The only person to be called who was connected with Knox was David Paterson, whose evidence had made a bad impression. Later he tried to justify his revelations in a letter to the *Caledonian Mercury* insisting that in only obeying his employer's orders, he had been made a scapegoat for Dr Knox.

Among the 55 witnesses listed, only 18 had been called to give evidence. What about Knox's three assistants, who were so closely connected with the delivery of the murder victims? The most plausible reason given for this omission was that had they been called, their testimonies would have revealed the contents of Hare's pre-trial statement and breached the court's agreement regarding his evidence.

Burke had been charged with only one murder, that of Mary Docherty or Campbell. Had the murders of Mary Paterson and James Wilson been included there would have been some remarkable and damning testimonies in court, especially from Mary Paterson's friend Janet Brown. Other singular omissions were Burke's brother Constantine, his wife Elizabeth and their two sons Richard and William, who if old enough to wear Daft Jamie's clothes must have been eligible to testify. Another vital witness would have been Elizabeth Main, the Hares' Irish ser-

vant, of whom Burke said: 'Hare's servant girl could give information respecting them murders in Hare's house, if she likes.'

The newspapers and broadsheets encouraged the public
opinion that the conviction of Burke would satisfy neither the
law nor the country, and that Hare must be brought to justice.
There was even some sympathy for Burke as 'another of Hare's
victims', as well as persistent suspicion of Knox. On 27 December
the *Caledonian Mercury* proclaimed:

> We are satisfied that the public do not know a tithe of the truth
> and that there are still hid more horrid things (if indeed that be
> possible) than those which have been revealed. An investigation
> of the most searching kind is due to the public and all the teach-
> ers of anatomy, within and without the University ought to be
> examined as to the manner in which they are accustomed to
> receive their subjects. And in particular, the students and assis-
> tants (during the last two sessions) of one gentleman whose
> name has unfortunately been too much mixed up with the late
> proceedings. Without a full and complete investigation, the
> public can have no guarantee that every anatomical teacher in
> Edinburgh has not a Burke in his pay at the moment. The pres-
> ent impression on the minds of the people is that one gentleman
> stands in the same relation to Burke that the murders of
> Macbeth did to Banquo.

It says little for human nature that less than £10 was collected
in a subscription raised for Mr and Mrs Gray, without whose
evidence Burke and Hare would have continued their murders
undetected. Their only reward the satisfaction of a clear

conscience, the Grays went to lodge in the Grassmarket, away from the crowds who swarmed daily over Burke's house (ignoring the landlord's attempts to charge an admission fee) to gape at the murder scene and collect souvenirs including rags and filthy bed straw. On 27 December the *Caledonian Mercury* provided a graphic account:

> Bloody straw in a corner, a heap of bloody clothes on the floor and a pile of old boots and shoes, amounting to several dozens (for which the miscreant's pretended trade of a shoemaker can never account) seem to us strong indications that the den of the monster now so justly condemned to die, has been the scene of manifold murders. Many have seen this horrid place and all have left it impressed with the same conviction.

Sir Walter Scott also visited the scene. A keen follower of the trial and never idle with his pen, he described the situation thus:

> We have the horrors of the west-port to amuse us, and that we may appear wiser than our neighbours, we drive in our carriages filled with well dress'd females to see the wretched cellars in which these atrocities were perpetrated and any one that can get a pair of shoes cobbled by Burke would preserve them with as much devotion as a Catholic would do the sandals of a saint which had pressed the holy soil of Palestine.

Sir Walter was also busy with plans to secure a seat to view the public execution; even such a revered and educated man was not immune to such entertainments at the time. As soon as the date was made public, tenants of the high 'lands' around the

Lawnmarket offered their windows for hire. Fashionable Edinburgh jostled for the best viewing positions.

In prison Burke was being treated for his 'embarrassing wound' (his testicular cancer). He was also, like many a criminal before and since, developing religious leanings. In his official confession, made on 3 January and published by the *Edinburgh Advertiser*, he had tried to implicate Hare as deeply as he could. Now he made a more detailed confession, including a list of the murders, to the *Edinburgh Evening Courant*. This was published on 7 February 1829. In this latest confession he declared that neither he nor Hare, as far as he knew, had supplied any subjects for dissection except those he had mentioned, and had never done so by raising dead bodies from the grave. He added that they had 'never allowed Dr Knox or his assistants to know exactly where their houses were, but Paterson, Dr Knox's porter or doorkeeper knew'. He and Hare always met with a ready market for the bodies, he said, and when they delivered one they were always told to get more.

But, he insisted, he was never a resurrection man. Mrs Burke and Mrs Hare were not present while the murders were committed (although later in the statement he said that Hare's wife often helped them to pack the murdered bodies into the boxes), and he claimed that he did not tell Helen Burke about the murders. He provided her with drink and better victuals without revealing the source of his income: his explanation to her was that he bought dead bodies and sold them on to the doctors. That was why they were called resurrection men in the West Port.

The days of Burke's incarceration turned into weeks. Although his statements exonerated Dr Knox from all blame, Burke still raged that the doctor owed him for the delivery of Mrs Docherty's body: the £5 would have provided him with better clothes to make a good impression on the scaffold.

THE EXECUTION

On 27 January, the eve of his execution, Burke with his ankles chained was taken by coach from Calton gaol to the lock-up in Liberton's Wynd off the Lawnmarket. The sound of hammering audible from his cell was no doubt a grim reminder of what lay in store: workmen were erecting barriers to keep spectators from the scaffold.

By 8 am the next morning, Wednesday 28 January, the largest crowd to have assembled in Edinburgh streets (estimated at 25,000 people) had gathered in spite of torrential rain (see plate 21). It included residents from neighbouring towns as well as Edinburgh locals, all closely wedged together with little breathing space, watching the scaffold and waiting in solemn silence for Burke to arrive on his last journey. Every window that could provide a glimpse of him or the scaffold was occupied, at a cost varying from 5s to £1, and some of the braver and more agile folk had taken to the rooftops for a better view.

In the lock-up Burke awoke at 5.30 am. His fetters were removed, at which he murmured 'So all my earthly chains fall! Oh, that the hour was come which shall separate me from this world.' An hour later two Catholic priests arrived and Burke left his cell with them. On the way to the keeper's room he accidentally met the executioner, telling him: 'I am not ready for you yet.' Taking a seat by the fire, he was given a glass of wine and drank 'Farewell to all my friends.' He received the priests' prayers for his soul, giving no acknowledgement or confession beyond a deep sigh.

At 8 am, with his arms pinioned, Burke was led out of Liberton Wynd in a small procession of magistrates and officers, with Father Reid at his side. Their appearance was greeted by the waiting crowds with one loud and simultaneous roar. This seemed to disconcert Burke for a moment, but when he reached the scaffold he responded to the shouts of derision with a look of fierce defiance before preparing to receive a last prayer from the priest.

His decision to kneel with his back towards the crowd infuriated those who had waited so long for this dramatic moment. There were angry shouts to those on the scaffold with him: 'Stand out of the way!' and 'Turn him round!' There were also shouts of 'Bring out Hare!' and 'Hang Hare!' Even Dr Knox did not escape the crowd's attention. 'Hang Knox! and 'He's a noxious morsel!' they cried.

Burke rose from his knees, lifted the silk handkerchief on which he had knelt and put it in his pocket, then glanced up to the gallows. At 8.10 am, as the executioner was adjusting the rope around his neck, Father Reid whispered: 'Say your creed and when you come to the words "Lord Jesus Christ" give the signal and die with his blessed name in your mouth.' But the priest could hardly be heard because of further shouts from the crowd of 'Burke him!' and 'Give him no rope!'

When the executioner was about to adjust the rope, Burke said to him, 'The knot's behind.' These were the last words he uttered. A few seconds later, in the early morning shadow of St Giles' Cathedral, he gave the signal. Amid the shouts of the crowd he died, only a slight movement of his feet providing entertainment for those who watched.

His body hung there for the best part of an hour. As it was being placed in a coffin, the crowd swarmed forward and were restrained from seizing it only by the police and the barriers. The workmen began to dismantle the scaffold, while people scrambled for souvenirs. Knives and scissors worked busily on the rope—pieces of which were subsequently to be sold for half a crown an inch—while the hangman was acclaimed as the hero of the hour. For those who lost out on the rope, even a handful of shavings from the coffin were preserved as a relic.

As the murderer's coffin disappeared from view, this was not quite the end. The law had not finished with William Burke.

CHAPTER FIVE

The Sordid Aftermath

As Burke made his last appearance on the dissecting table for which he had provided so many corpses, everyone clamoured to see the body. The crowds had been pouring towards Surgeon's Square since daybreak that Thursday morning, hammering on the classroom door and demanding admission. Dr Monro's regular students were provided with tickets, but even with the assistance of the police, it was difficult to restrain those who wanted to fight their way in.

The murderer's brain was the subject of the lecture. The top of his head was sawn off; according to a contemporary report by Thomas Ireland in *West Port Murders*:

> the amount of blood that gushed out was enormous, and by the time the lecture was finished which was not until three o'clock (it had begun at one), the area of the lecture-room had the appearance of a butcher's slaughter-house from its flowing down and being trodden upon.

In the meantime, students who had failed to get in for the beginning of the demonstration were at the door demanding admittance. The police used their batons to preserve order.

Fights broke out between police and students and considerable damage was done to the windows on either side of the anatomical theatre. At 4 pm, Professor Christison appeared and tried to restore calm by announcing that he had arranged admission to the lecture room for all medical students, 50 at a time, to view the remains after Dr Monro had finished his dissections. The satisfied crowd dispersed with cheers, both police and students nursing injuries.

On Friday, the general public was admitted from an early hour to view the murderer's corpse. It was estimated that 25,000 people (the same number as had attended the execution) assembled for this unique opportunity. As long as daylight lasted, a constant stream was admitted by one stair to file past the corpse—the shaved head of which showed continuous stitching where the skull had been replaced, with signs of blood—and to exit by the opposite stair. The presence of several women among the spectators (and also at the execution) provoked adverse comment in the press.

When the doors finally closed, the business of the doctors and students began in earnest. The flesh was stripped from the bones and Burke's skeleton preserved. Apart from Burke's official and *Courant* confessions, still to be published (on 6 and 7 February), the story was almost over.

But not quite. The crimes had been of such enormity that Burke's execution and dissection was far from sufficient to satisfy the public. There were others on whom they wanted to vent their anger in the name of justice, and Hare was top of the list. Most people, especially those who had glimpsed his sinister demeanour in court, suspected that he was the ringleader who had lured the victims into his den and performed the actual killings. At the trial, far from showing remorse, he had seemed rather pleased with himself for betraying his partner and sending him to the gallows.

Whatever the opinion of the people and the press—also not slow to name Hare—the Lord Advocate knew that he was faced with a tricky situation. He was quite aware that had it not been for Hare's testimony the verdict on Burke would have been 'Not proven', and Burke would have walked free.

Daft Jamie's mother and sister—who were bringing a private prosecution for Jamie's murder—petitioned that Hare be kept in prison in case he seized the opportunity of fleeing to Ireland. A subscription to pay for the costs was raised by a sympathetic public, urged on by the press. The Wilsons' petition was considered, but Hare had kept his part of the bargain; it was argued that if the Crown went back on the agreement and kept him in gaol pending a civil prosecution, he would not have a fair trial, and the public would lose faith in the integrity of the law. (Not that the public cared a jot about such niceties: all they wanted was to see Hare hanged.)

In the meantime Maggie Hare was released. With her child in her arms she went back to Tanner's Close, but was soon recognized and followed by a mob pelting her with stones and mud.

Like Helen Burke she was rescued by the police, who locked her up again overnight for her own safety. She then made her way to Glasgow but was again recognized and had to take refuge in a prison cell, from which she roundly cursed Hare for her predicament. All she wished, she said, was to cross the channel with her bairn and end her days in her own country. At last she was smuggled aboard the *Fingal*, which was to leave Greenock for Belfast on 12 February. This was not quite the last heard of her. Rumour identified her in the unlikely role of a Mrs Hare employed as a nursemaid in Paris some thirty years later.

Back in Edinburgh the Wilsons reluctantly withdrew their warrant against Hare. The case was closed and Hare was free. Penniless and homeless, he knew the sooner he left Edinburgh the better, for if starvation didn't kill him the mob thirsting for his blood certainly would. He left Calton gaol at 8 pm on 5 February 1929 and, accompanied by Sergeant Fisher, was taken by hackney carriage to meet the southbound mail coach at Newington. Wearing a hat pulled well over his eyes and wrapped in an old coat, he must have looked out of the window with some dread as they passed Dr Knox's house. As Hare climbed on to an outside seat on the coach, the sergeant, for all to hear, wished 'Mr Black' a safe journey home.

Twenty miles further down the road at Noblehouse, as the passengers were set down at an inn, Hare was recognized by one of the passengers inside the coach. This was none other than Douglas Sandford, junior counsel for the Wilsons. When

Hare tried to take an inside seat Sandford objected and, watching him retreat to the freezing cold once more, revealed his identity to the other passengers.

News of the notorious passenger travelled ahead of the coach. By the time it reached Dumfries a huge crowd was waiting outside the King's Arms in the High Street. Only the intervention of 100 special constables, with batons at the ready, combined with the safety offered by the town gaol, saved Hare from the 800-strong mob gathered to lynch him. Frustrated at his escape from justice at their hands, the crowd attempted to break down the prison doors. When they were beaten off, they vented their rage by smashing windows and lamps.

Early the next morning Hare was smuggled out of the gaol, escorted to the Annan Road and left to cross the border into England. A reported sighting in Carlisle was his last known whereabouts, but a Victorian tale later identified a blind beggar sitting at the corner of London's Oxford Street as Hare. The story went that his identity had been discovered by a workman, and that he had been thrown into a lime pit and blinded.

Dr Knox's biographer Henry Lonsdale told another story: that Hare and his wife had returned to their native country and were heard of no more, except in the pages of fiction, until in 1870 Hare was seen in London.

While the populace of Edinburgh clamoured for Hare to be hung in chains, the future of another man hung equally uneasily in the balance. Dr Knox was a more readily accessible scapegoat;

his misfortune was to have been in the wrong place when Burke and Hare were seeking a recipient for their first corpse. The public demanded to know why Knox had not been called as a witness at Burke's trial; he could have provided evidence to prevent Hare escaping the hangman's rope. Knox took refuge in a dignified silence, holding public opinion in contempt. He was determined to conduct business as usual, and planned to attend a meeting of the Royal Society arranged by Sir Walter Scott, where he was to read an essay on dissection. Outraged, Scott recorded in his *Journal*:

> A bold proposal truly from one who has had so lately the bold-
> ness of trading so deep in human flesh. I will oppose his reading
> in the present circumstances if I should stand alone, but I hope
> he will be wrought upon to withdraw his essay or postpone it at
> least. It is very bad taste to push himself forward just now.

Presumably many members agreed with him. Scott was to add with evident relief that the reading would be postponed.

Worse was to come for Dr Knox. In February a committee of gentlemen headed by the Marquis of Queensberry investigated in the public interest Knox's dealings with Burke and Hare. Was Knox guilty of criminal negligence in not suspecting the pair's foul play or asking about the origin of their corpses? Remember, these included a young boy and three other healthy young people: Mary Paterson, James Wilson and Ann McDougal, who had died prematurely and mysteriously. It was not well received that Dr Knox had quickly disfigured Daft

Jamie's corpse on learning that it might be recognized. If Knox believed that packages delivered by Burke and Hare were generally the bodies of old derelicts who had died of drink or natural causes, handed over by friends and family who could not afford a burial, what were his thoughts about the 12-year-old boy and his grandmother brought to Surgeon's Square packed tightly into a barrel?

That such matters should be investigated was good news for the crowd that assembled on Calton Hill bearing a life-size effigy of Knox (now termed the 'obnoxious anatomist'). It set off down Waterloo Place, over Waverley Bridge, to South Bridge and past the equally notorious Surgeon's Square, gathering reinforcements as it marched. Its destination was 4 Newington Place. There, in Knox's garden, the furious crowd yelled for him to appear and hung his effigy from a tree. An attempt to burn it failed, so it was hacked to pieces instead. Knox escaped by the back door, wearing an old military cloak and armed with sword and pistol. Seeking refuge with his friend Dr Adams, he said: 'Had I been called upon to defend myself, I could have measured a score of the brutes.' Meanwhile the frustrated mob, restrained by the police, had to be content with throwing stones which broke windows and injured some of the constables.

The riots became a daily occurrence. Crowds gathered in the Canongate, High Street and Surgeon's Square. Rumour circulated that Knox had fled to Portobello, so another effigy was carried there to be hung from an ancient gibbet in Tower Street and burnt. Knox's house, however, was still the main target. There were many arrests but few convictions; orders to pay fines were met from a sympathetic fund set up for the purpose.

The press, realizing that they were unlikely to ever get another story like this one, daily repeated a warning that public agitation would never subside until the city was relieved of Dr Knox's presence or his innocence was proved. On 31 December 1828 the *Edinburgh Weekly Chronicle* commented:

> It is lamentable to think that the practise of a science, designed for the preservation of human life should, through the avidity of any individual to possess subjects, have directly tended to encourage its profuse destruction. In purchasing the bodies there must have been an utter recklessness — a thorough indifference as to causes and consequences, which in point of criminality very closely borders guilty knowledge.

The fact remains that Knox's carefully maintained silence was his undoing. Had he expressed shock and remorse at the revelations concerning Burke and Hare, and regret that he had failed to suspect murder, had he taken responsibility for this omission by pleading that he had made a grave error of judgement, then there might have been rumblings of sympathy from the public. But now, fanned by the press, public disquiet spread nationwide, leading to attacks on medical students in other parts of Scotland and in England.

In his lecture room Knox continued his demonstrations, ever present and punctual. When his loyal students were distracted by the angry crowds outside, he told them to keep calm. 'It is my life they seek, not yours,' he said, according to Henry Lonsdale, adding that the protesters were 'too cowardly to confront such a body of gentlemen as I see before me'.

Meanwhile the committee appointed to investigate Dr Knox's role in the murder—from which Lord Queensberry had withdrawn, for reasons unstated—reported that after an extensive examination of evidence 'in the course of which they had courted information from every quarter', they had seen no evidence that Knox or his assistants knew that murder had been committed when they procured any of the subjects brought to his rooms. Knox was mildly reproved for the circumstances in which his assistants and doorkeeper accepted bodies from suppliers they believed to be body snatchers; the instructions from Dr Knox not to enquire about the bodies' origins were deemed 'incautious' and requiring 'greater vigilance'.

This supposedly private report came to the ears of the press. On 17 March Knox wrote a long letter to the *Caledonian Mercury* enclosing the report and protesting

> that every effort has been made to convert my misfortune into positive and intended personal guilt of the most dreadful character. Scarcely any individual has ever been the object of more systematic and atrocious attacks than I have been. Nobody acquainted with this place requires to be told from what quarters these have proceeded.
>
> This is the very first time I have ever made any statement to

the public in my own vindication, and it shall be the last. It would
be unjust to the authors of the former calumnies to suppose
that they would not renew them now. I can only assure them
that, as far as I am concerned, they will renew them in vain.

These remarks show that he blamed the personal vendetta
against him by his erstwhile doorkeeper David Paterson for
some of his troubles. Paterson tried to enlist the support of Sir
Walter Scott by suggesting that Scott write a book on Burke
and Hare for which he, David Paterson, would offer his invaluable collection of anecdotes. His offer was given short shrift by
Scott. Paterson's moment of glory had passed, although according to Andrew Leighton he bounced back in 1860 as a 'respectable citizen of Edinburgh'.

Although Dr Knox continued to go daily to his lecture room,
his social life was over. Respectable middle-class Edinburgh
closed its doors on him and, as many of its members were the
parents of his students and paid their fees, his numbers dimin-
ished as students chose instead the medical schools in Glasgow
or Dublin. Knox faced a bleak future attended by moments of
dread that he would be pointed out on the streets as the notorious anatomist. Failing to secure the Chair of Pathology at
Edinburgh University, he took an appointment as an extra-
mural lecturer, but his reputation went before him and he could
no longer attract enough students. When the final blow was
delivered and Knox was struck off the Roll of Fellows of the
Royal Society, he left Edinburgh, disposing of his school in

Surgeon's Square to his former pupil and future biographer Henry Lonsdale. He spent time teaching in Glasgow at the Portland Street School, but his class was so small that he returned the fees to the pupils.

It was soon apparent that no university would appoint Knox to a chair and no medical school in Scotland would welcome him. In London, he fared no better. According to Professor Christison he was employed as 'a lecturer, demonstrator or showman to a travelling party of Ojibbeway Indians', a somewhat inaccurate description of the work that went into one of his subsequent and most eminent publications, *Ethnology, or the Races of Man.*

Fate had not spared Knox's private life. His wife, that woman unknown in Edinburgh society, died in 1841 after giving birth to their sixth child, and soon afterwards their four-year-old son also died. The future was to hold little for Knox beyond several publications, produced while he struggled in vain to return to his old life. Finally, at the age of 63, he obtained an appointment as pathological anatomist at the London Cancer Hospital and, his past mercifully unknown, opened a practice in 9 Lambe Terrace, Hackney, living there with his only surviving son Edward and his sister Mary. Lonsdale wrote that he did 'a great deal in the obstetrical department', forgoing fees and often providing food for his poorer patients.

Knox died of apoplexy on 20 December 1862, aged 71, and was buried at Woking Cemetery. The obituaries were on the whole generous and refrained from mentioning the connection with Burke and Hare, while many of the medical establishment believed that he had been a victim of professional jealousy and made a scapegoat by his peers.

It is appropriate to end this account with a touching story Lonsdale tells of the man he respected as a genius but who was also compassionate and kind-hearted wherever humanity was concerned. Walking in the Edinburgh Meadows with his friend Dr Adams, Knox was very taken with a pretty little six-year-old girl playing nearby:

> He gave her a penny and said, 'Now, my dear, you and I will be friends. Would you come and live with me if you got a whole penny every day?' 'No,' said the child, 'you would maybe sell me to Dr Knox.' The anatomist started back with a painfully stunned expression, his features began to twitch convulsively and tears appeared in his eyes.

BURKE AND HARE'S LEGACY

The infamy of Burke and Hare gave a new word to the dictionary: 'to burke', meaning to smother. And of course the authorities feared copycat cases. As the *Evening Weekly Chronicle* asked: 'Can it be doubted that there are many miscreants who when they become possessed of Burke and Hare's fearful secret will not hesitate a moment, if there is a prospect of impunity, to murder a fellow creature in order to convert or coin his body into ten sovereigns?' There were in fact later instances of murders carried out in order to supply anatomists, such as the killing of the 'Italian boy' in 1831 by London burkers John Bishop and Thomas Williams (see plate 22).

The Anatomy Act of 1832, which 'provided for executors and other people legally in charge of dead bodies to give them to licensed surgeons and teachers of anatomy unless the deceased had expressed conscientious objection to being dissected', put an end to all secret supply to anatomical schools in Great Britain and Ireland. Directly resulting from the scandal of Dr Knox's 'incautious and unfortunate conduct', it brought to an end the activities of body snatchers and grave robbers, allowing the dead to rest in peace.

Nearly 200 years later, the case continues to horrify and fascinate in equal measure. It has had numerous fictional outings: in addition to Dylan Thomas's play *The Doctor and the Devils*, Burke and Hare have provided many novelists with ready-made plots. The earliest example was Robert Louis Stevenson's *The Body Snatcher*, written in 1881 and 'laid aside in a justifiable disgust' with Dr Wolfe Macfarlane, a thinly disguised Knox. Stevenson was paid £30 for it but when men wearing sandwich boards paraded through the streets of London to protest, displaying posters so gruesome that they were suppressed by the police, he wrote that he had 'long condemned the story as an offence against good manners' (Alanna Knight, *The Robert*

Louis Stevenson Treasury, Shepheard-Walwyn, 1985). In more recent times two very readable fictional accounts of Burke and Hare, *Rest without Peace* and *The Search for Maggie Hare* (Macmillan, 1974, 1976) were written by Edinburgh-based author Elizabeth Byrd. The Burke and Hare case has also inspired a spate of movies of the Hammer horror variety. In production even as this book goes to press is Irvine Welsh's feature film *The Meat Trade*, a modern version of the story set in Edinburgh in 2007.

As the curtains close on Scotland's most notorious serial murderers, there are still questions destined to remain unanswered. The most chilling is whether there were more murders than the 16 that Burke confessed to, bearing in mind the many frantic appeals made to the police during 1828 by the friends and relations of missing people. On 29 December, the *Caledonian Mercury* claimed that:

> In the course of the last two years Burke now states he sold to one individual from thirty to forty uninterred bodies, the conclusion is inevitable that he and his associates must have committed many murders! ... It has been remarked that numbers of the unfortunate females upon the town have lately disappeared, no one knew how. Natural deaths have become rarer among that class and for some time past the interment of one of them has scarcely been heard of. Abandoned by the relatives and friends whom they dishonoured, and excluded from all notice or regard by the virtuous part of society, there was none

to care for and none to inquire what had become of them. The
girl Paterson was one of them ... but not the only one.

Hare's confession seemed to confirm Burke's body count, however; it 'disclosed nearly the same in point of number'. Of
considerable interest is what happened to this confession. The
disappearance of such an important document suggests that it
was deliberately destroyed, perhaps as part of the deal struck
with Hare. And what of those other witnesses who were never
called at Burke's trial, including Knox's three assistants? Was
this also done to spare Hare, or even Knox?

Another question is whether the later murders could have
been prevented. Edinburgh at that time had a less than ener-
getic police force, more inclined to use its batons than its brains,
and a class system where the rich and socially superior were
revered. If Knox's three assistants or the doctor himself had
gone to the police with suspicions about the body of Mary
Paterson, their views would have carried much weight: several
other lives would have been saved and Knox would have been
proclaimed a hero instead of a villain. But many of those who
may have suspected Burke and Hare belonged to Edinburgh's
underclass: they would have been reluctant to go to the police
because their own activities did not bear scrutiny, and because
they did not expect to receive justice for their kind. Living on
the vulnerable margins, such people were easy prey for the
murderers who, for several terrifying months, stalked the dark
city streets.

Sources & Reading

The National Archives of Scotland has the High Court minute book
and book of adjournal entries for the Burke trial, the indictment
against Burke and McDougal, and a prison record for the Burkes and
Hares — as well as petitions for their arrests for the murders of Mary
Docherty, James Wilson and Mary Paterson. At the National Library
of Scotland you can see contemporary published material on the case,
including broadsides and illustrations. At the Museum of the Royal
College of Surgeons of Edinburgh relics such as Burke's skeleton are
exhibited.

Those who would like to read a fuller account of the trial of
Burke and his official and *Courant* confessions should see William
Roughead's *Notable British Trials* (Wm Hodge, London, 1921). Also
recommended are Brian Bailey's *Burke and Hare: The Year of the
Ghouls* (Mainstream, 2005) and *Knox the Anatomist* by Isobel Rae
(Oliver & Boyd, 1964). Some other useful publications quoted in this
book are listed here.

H. Arnot, *History of Edinburgh* (Edinburgh, 1779)
J.B. Atlay, *Famous Trials of the Century* (London, 1899)
J. Bridie, *The Anatomist* (London, 1930)
T. Brown, *A New Guide to the City of Edinburgh* (*Caledonian Mercury*, 1792)
E. Burt, *Letters from a Gentleman in the North of Scotland*
    (London, 1815)
R. Chambers, *Reekiana, or Minor Antiquities of Edinburgh* (Edinburgh,
    1833)

R. Chambers, *Traditions of Edinburgh* (Edinburgh, 1825)

R. Christison, *The Life of Sir Robert Christison, Bart* (Blackwood & Sons, 1885)

H. Cockburn, *Memorials of his Time* (A & C Black, 1856)

Dictionary of National Biography

Echoes of Surgeon's Square, letter to the Lord Advocate (published as pamphlet, 1829)

Edinburgh Evening Courant

Edinburgh Weekly Chronicle

O. Dudley Edwards, *Burke and Hare* (Polygon, 1980)

B.D. Horn, *A Short History of the University of Edinburgh* (Edinburgh, 1967)

A. Law, *Education in Edinburgh in the Eighteenth Century* (Edinburgh, 1965)

A. Leighton, *The Court of Casus* (Houston & Wright, 1861)

J.G. Lockhart, *Memoirs of Sir Walter Scott* (A & C Black, 1869)

H. Lonsdale, *A Sketch of the Life and Writings of Robert Knox the Anatomist* (Macmillan, 1870)

J. Moores Ball, *The Sack'em Up Men*, (London, 1928)

Sir W. Scott, *Journal* (Oliver & Boyd, 1950)

T.C. Smout, *A History of the Scottish People 1560–1830* (Collins, 1969)

J. Taylor, *A Journey to Edenborough* (Edinburgh, 1903)

J. Wilson writing as 'Christopher North', *Blackwood's Edinburgh Magazine*, 1829

PICTURE ACKNOWLEDGEMENTS

The Publishers would like to thank the following for permission to use images in this book: akg-images **1**, The Royal College of Surgeons of Edinburgh **10**, **19**, **20**, The National Archives **22**, The National Archives of Scotland **14**, **15**, **17**, The National Library of Scotland **3**, **5**, **8**, **9**, **11**, **13**, **16**, **18**, **21**. Other images are from William Roughead's *Notable British Trials* (London, 1921).

Index

―――